Complete Dog Training For Beginners

Raise The Perfect Puppy in 30 Days!

2 Books in 1

Brianna Ramirez

THIS COLLECTION INCLUDES THE FOLLOWING BOOKS:

Complete Dog Training Workbook For Beginners:
Raise The Perfect Puppy in 30 Days!

Complete Mental Exercises for Dogs Handbook:
20+ Exercises to Stimulate Your Dog's Mind and Boost Mental Health!

Table of Contents

~~$25~~ FREE BONUS

House Train Your New Pup Today!

Scan QR code above to claim your free bonus!

OR

visit bit.ly/vipdogbonus

Ready to Keep a Tidy House & A Happy Pup?

Inside this included ebook for new dog parents, you'll find:

- ✓ **The simple way to housebreak any dog - guaranteed... even if they're disobedient at first!**
- ✓ **Guided instructions for both dog parents who are at home more, and busy parents who are unable to be home all day.**
- ✓ **How to identify your dog's natural temperament to accelerate the housebreaking process!**

Scan QR code above to claim your free bonus!

OR

visit bit.ly/vipdogbonus

BOOK 1

Complete Dog Training Workbook For Beginners

Raise The Perfect Puppy in 30 Days!

Brianna Ramirez

Book 1 Description

Learn how to teach your dog basic manners and skills in this effective 4-week course!

Don't you **hate** it when your dog chews on your shoes?

Are you **frustrated** when your dog barks for no reason?

Do you want your dog to be **patient and obedient** and especially not pull on the leash when you go for walks?

If you answer "**yes**" to any of these, then this book is for you. Dog training is simpler than you might assume. You certainly don't have to be a professional dog trainer to teach your dog basic skills. In fact, **it is a walk in the park.** All it takes is consistency, repetition, and a bit of know-how.

Certified and expert dog trainer, Brianna Ramirez, provides you with a **comprehensive, easy-to-follow, step-by-step guide** to help your pup adjust to their new home. All the training in this book follows a positivity-centric approach known as positive reinforcement. Not only it is a tried-and-true method of dog training, but it also enhances the bond between you and your canine companion.

In **Complete Dog Training Workbook For Beginners**, you'll discover:

- Basic (but bizarre) dog behaviors and how they are okay
- How to find the right dog for you
- How to prepare your home for your pup's arrival
- How to potty and crate train your pup
- Basic commands to teach your dog such as sit, stay, come, and down
- Effective strategies to deal with your dog chewing shoes
- What to do when your dog starts barking for no reason
- Strategic use of treats
- Easy ways to instill patience and discipline
- ... And so much more!

You can achieve all of this through **the power of positive reinforcement**. This training method is designed to be **humane** and **rewarding**, both for you and your dog. In fact, your dog will be **super excited** and **eager to learn** thanks to the methods highlighted in this book.

Imagine how much easier your life will be when your dog is happy and well-mannered. Through positive reinforcement, even dogs that you think cannot be reasoned with, can acclimate to their new home. Through this 4-week course, **you too can bring out the best in your dog**.

Overcome all dog-related problems with **Complete Dog Training Workbook For Beginners**.

Introduction

"Dogs do speak, but only to those who know how to listen."

- Orhan Pamuk

We all want to provide the best care for our furry friends. We feed them, make sure they stay on top of vaccinations, maintain tip-top hygiene, and soon. But you might find that even with your utmost care, it's hard to teach them proper manners and discipline. Maybe your pup misbehaves or does their business on the rug when they should be doing their #1 and #2 outside. But you know that violence is never the answer, so you are a little lost. Or maybe you are getting a pup soon and want them to have a great start. Well, look no further!

Complete Dog Training Workbook for Beginners: Raise The Perfect Puppy in 30 Days! is the perfect book to help you better understand your cute companion and help them acclimate to their new life.

Equipped with the know-how from this book, you will not only learn about dog psychology and behavior but also how you can utilize that to cultivate good habits through positive reinforcement.

You might not realize it, but your work as a dog owner starts way before bringing one home. You need to make preparations to welcome your new companion, and we will go over exactly what you need to do. This is particularly important if you have not raised a dog before.

In this book, you will understand exactly why dogs behave a certain way, especially if it is a bad thing, like digging for no reason or howling in the middle of the day. With this knowledge, you will start to understand why some training methods work and others do not.

In addition, there are useful skills and habits that your dog needs to develop as early as possible to make their life and yours easier in various scenarios. We will cover all of that in detail and provide you with step-by-step instructions.

Of course, you will also learn how to handle bad behaviors. Yes, harming your dog, be it physically or psychologically, is never okay. This is why we will go over more productive methods to curb bad habits which is harmless to your pup.

Yes, we have a lot to cover in this book, but to help you better grasp the subject and to make reviewing easier, all of the content will be summarized at the end of the chapter. That way, you can double-check that you understand everything that's being said so far and you can revisit the review section in the future if you ever need a refresher in the future.

My name is Brianna Ramirez,and I have been around animals ever since I could remember. Chief among them are dogs, which I really admire. I am not saying that cats or rabbits are inferior in any way, but there is just something about a dog's love that stuck with me.

I have many fond memories of dogs, but one stands out. It made me rethink my career path and life direction in general. It was a Golden Retriever called Runt, on account that he was indeed the runt of the litter.

He was a very dear friend to me when I was young. He was playful, maybe a little too playful, energetic, and a bit clumsy. I think he's a psychic as well because it felt like he knew what I was thinking all the time.

I remember going through my first heartbreak in a romantic relationship. Runt did not give me a pat on the back and tell me, "Oh, there are plenty of fishes in the sea," since he was a dog. Instead, he licked my face and tried to sit on my lap, or my face, I couldn't tell until a minute later.

Through my first failed job interview, being betrayed by the people I thought were my friends, and other tragedies, Runt was there for me. He couldn't talk, but I could see it in his eyes that no matter what happened, he still loved me without question.

Every day, rain and dry, Runt would wait for me at the door, tail wagging, in frequency when he could hear me walking up the steps. He jumped on me as soon as the door flung open and was always a welcomed sight whenever I was feeling drained from the world.

And that got me thinking. Dogs do not have that big of a brain and they cannot possibly comprehend the complexity of the world. Their hearts are even smaller, and yet it is a bottomless well from which they draw unlimited love. No matter who you are, no matter how much of a failure you think you are, your dog loves you all the same.

So, I cannot, in my good conscience, not reward such unquestioned affection. Since then, I have devoted my life to dog training. My passion for these lovable pups put me on this path, but nothing could prepare me for the challenge I face. But I learned a lot on the job and made many wonderful memories along the way.

People bring their dogs to me because they want the best for their pups, and I am certain you do as well. Worry not, I will share with you what I have learned working with these adorable puppies so you can have the best time with them and give them the best life they could ever ask for.

Though I wish dogs could talk so we can better understand and accommodate them, they could not. So, like our dogs, we just have to show our intention and affection through actions.

While it is best to start training your dog when it is still a young pup, you can still apply the exercises in this book on older mutts. Contrary to popular belief, you can indeed teach old dogs new tricks.

After having read this book, you will not believe how much progress your furry friend makes in such a short time.

The best time to begin is now! Don't delay, start your 30-day dog training **today!**

Chapter 1: How Your Furry Friend Perceives the World

"Did you know that there are over 300 words for love in canine?"

– Gabriel Zevin

Have you ever wondered why people call their dogs "fur babies"? Though the common answer is that they just love their dogs like their children, there is a good scientific reason why this term can be somewhat accurate

A wave of new research shed light on how dogs really see the world. I will not bore you with the details, and you might already know this, but dogs process and respond to stimuli the same way as a child.

In other words, dogs are literally furry babies.

Just like children, dogs enjoy our attention. Just like children, you have a significant impact on their development and emotional state

What is also interesting is that dogs do certain things for a reason. Yes, eating grass or gnawing on a rock looks silly, but they have a reason for doing that. You see, dogs experience the world very similarly to how children do when they are in the "oral fixation stage." It is a fancy way of saying that they understand the world through their mouth – by tasting everything.

Does it make sense? Not to us, but it is why dogs eat grass.

Although sometimes, it is not curiosity but a coping mechanism. Just like humans, dogs do experience anxiety, and chewing on grass might be one way to cope with it. We, of course, do not do that. Some of us just eat a tub of ice cream instead.

I also want to point out that, smart as humans are, we do have a fair share of silly moments in our lives. A quick search on YouTube will show a gazillion proofs of humans' lapses of judgment.

Just like humans, dogs also make mistakes. They have their serious moments where they save lives from a bear attack and silly moments when they can't even catch the ball.

Dogs can also tell when we are happy.

Research also tells us that dogs also look at humans in the eyes and follow our eye movements, similar to 6-month-old children. Another study found that dogs learned to recognize a happy face better than a sad face. Now, this part is not proven yet, but I think they have a better response to happy faces because they see a lot more happy faces than sad ones. Who can be sad when there is a dog in the room?

Why do dogs look guilty? There is also a reason for

that. Except the answer is that they know that they did wrong. An adult dog, according to research, has a mind that is roughly similar to a child who is two and a half years old.

That means dogs do not develop complex emotions such as guilt. So, why do they look guilty when after they expelled on the rug? Well, they do not feel guilt, but they do feel joy, fear, anger, love, and disgust.

So, the look your dog gave you when you caught it red-handed was not guilt, but fear. It is its basic fear of punishment.

So, what does all of this tell us?

It means that **we are still scratching the surface** when it comes to an understanding our canine companions. Again, it would be really convenient if we can ask them questions like humans, but animals cannot talk. So, we have to find ways to "ask" the right questions so we can deepen our understanding.

For dog owners like us, it tells us that dogs think and behave like children. You would not hit your kid if they had an accident on the rug, so the same logic applies to dogs.

Try to see the world as if you are a toddler, and maybe some of your dog's behaviors start to make sense in their way.

Other Common Behaviors

With that in mind, let us look at other common canine behaviors and the possible reasons behind them.

The Head Tilt

Dogs tilt their head to the side as if they are asking us a question, and this assumption is correct 99% of the time. Dogs tilt their head when they see something they don't really understand or something that they have not seen before.

Sometimes, your dog may tilt their head to get a better view. Unlike ours, a dog's nose does get in the way, and one way to get around this persistent obstruction is a head tilt. Sometimes, the ear flap can muffle sounds, so dogs tilt their head to hear better as well.

The Tail Chase

This is a sight every dog owner is familiar with. Your dog runs around in circles, chasing its tail. Does it look silly? Yes. Does your dog know that it is silly? Probably. Tail-chasing is natural and dogs sometimes do this when they are feeling playful.

That said, there could be an underlying problem if your dog chews on its tail. If this behavior is constant and intense, it could be a sign of OCD. Yes, dogs can have OCD as well. You should consult a vet if this behavior persists since it could lead to injury.

Howling, Barking, or Baying

Dogs have to vocalize sometimes. Barking is normal for dogs,and some do love the sound of their voice more than others. Dogs howl, bark, or bay as a way to communicate with their fellow dogs as well as humans.

Your dog may bark when they sense danger. That can be a stranger coming to the front door, a squirrel in the backyard, or a bear.

As for howling, it is an instinctive and contagious behavior. The closest example is that we tend to yawn when we see other people yawning. Dogs will howl if they hear other dogs howl. How dogs respond to howling depends on the breed. Some will bay or howl, others just let out a yip.

But howling has to start somewhere. Someone has to start this chain, right? One reason why dogs howl could be distress or just plain boredom. Curbing excessive vocalization can be tricky, but I will tell you how to handle that in a later chapter.

Leaning

Some dogs love to lean on people, especially their owners. What is interesting is that this behavior is more common in giant dog breeds. Your dog may do it not because it can't support itself, but because they want to be closer to you. Think of it like a subtle hug.

Dogs are affectionate creatures, after all. One common misconception here is that leaning is a sign that your dog is trying to assert dominance over you. That is not true.

Digging

There are many possible reasons why your dog would dig up the yard. The most common one is that they are just bored or anxious. Sometimes, they make holes in the ground so they can hide toys or other possessions from other dogs or perceived threats.

If it is a hot summer day, then your dog just wants to make a cool hole to lie down in because the surface of the ground might be hot, but the earth underneath is nice and cold.

This habit can become annoying for the owners, so if you are somebody who doesn't enjoy digging in their backyard you will have to take intentional steps to curb that kind of behavior. Again, I will tell you exactly how in a later chapter.

The Butt Sniff

This behavior, though bizarre, is normal, and there is scientific reasoning behind this. You see, dogs have a far superior olfactory system. They can smell about 10,000 times better than humans.

In addition to putting everything in their mouths, dogs also learn about the world with their noses. In fact, when presented with a foreign object, dogs tend to use their nose first before their mouth.

So, when two dogs meet and start sniffing each other's rear, that is basically an interview. Most of the scents are concentrated in the area of the anus, and genitals and dogs can learn a lot just by taking a whiff or two. They can learn about gender, temperament, reproductive status, diet, and much more from around 15 seconds of sniffing.

What is also fascinating is the fact that everything has a unique scent that a dog can discern. If your dog starts to sniff people, they are just trying to understand them better.

So, there really is no reason why you should prevent two dogs from sniffing each other. They can get along better if they know each other better, and one quick way for that is to let them get a whiff.

Humping

Although this behavior is present during mating, it is not always sexual. Your dog may even hump objects and people in addition to other dogs. It is also not a sign of dominance.

If it is not mating, then it is just part of their normal play. Your dog may just be excited or want your attention. Humping between spayed or neutered dogs is usually okay but can lead to mating between unaltered dogs.

Humping objects is also okay unless it bothers you or if your dog does it excessively. But humping people should be discouraged, and we will go over how in a bit.

Key Takeaways

In the first chapter, we delve into common canine behaviors and dispel some common misconceptions. Let's do a quick recap:

- Dogs are a lot like very young children – they don't know right from wrong so you have to teach them the difference
- Dogs use their nose and mouth to understand the world around them
- Never attribute to a dog's malice that, which can be explained by its boredom
- There are no bad dogs, just misunderstood pups who haven't been trained properly
- There is a reason behind everything they do, no matter how ridiculous the reason may be to humans

Coming up in the next chapter, we will talk about the best training methodology: positive reinforcement.

Chapter 2: How and Why Positive Reinforcement Works

"A dog is the only thing on earth that loves you more than you love yourself." – Josh Billings

Positive reinforcement uses a reward system to encourage good and desired behavior. This system works for pretty much everything with a functioning brain, making it very effective for both animals and humans.

Here's an example. If you get $10 every time you get an A on your report card, you would want to get an A, right?

The only difference with dogs is the reward. Instead of giving them cash to buy treats, you give them treats, toys, praise, or anything that your dog finds rewarding to reinforce desired behaviors.

Flip the script, and you have a powerful way to curb bad behaviors as well. You just do not give them the rewards, and they will eventually stop.

While I will go into detail about certain behaviors in this book, you can apply the practices in this chapter to teach your dog other tricks and behaviors.

The reward system is used to encourage dogs to repeat

the behavior, making it an effective tool for shaping your dog's behavior. It is that simple but to make the most of it, there are some basic guidelines you need to follow.

Timing

You need to time it right. That means **you must reward your dog immediately or within seconds of desired behavior**. Dogs live in the present, and if you wait too long, they may not associate the reward with the behavior.

For instance, if you tell your dog to sit but only reward them after they have stood up, guess what? They think that they are rewarded for standing.

This is also why it is just plain wrong to use violence when your dog messed up your house. Not only does that make you a horrible person, but your dog just does not understand why they got punished in the first place since the punishment is detached in time from the misbehavior. They do not know any better.

Keep it Short

Although dogs use their nose and mouth to investigate, **they use body language primarily to communicate**. This is how I teach dogs different commands and tricks. First, I get them to perform the action before pinning a short command (one word or two at most) to it.

Here's an example. If I have to teach a dog how to sit, this is how I would normally approach it. I would take a toy or treat, make sure the dog has its eyes on it, and move it slightly behind their head so they have to sit and look up to see it. When they are sitting, I lower my hand and put the treat or toy close to the ground between their front paws to encourage them into a down position.

And I don't pin the command immediately. I just get the pup to repeat the behavior first before throwing in the command "sit" or "down" in a calm voice. I don't repeat the word and I keep the verbal cues short and simple.

You will just confuse your dog if you say, "Runt, I want you to be a good boy and sit for me" every time you want your dog to sit down. Although Runt learned the "sit" command and will sit down when I said it to him, guesswhat? He would have understood only two words from that sentence: Runt (his name) and sit (the command). So, keep it short.

Consistency

In the same vein of keeping everything simple, maintain consistency. That means, **use the same cues and stick to them** lest you confuse your pup. Everyone in the family must remember the specifics. Put up a list of cues if you have to.

This brings me to another half of my training. Remember how dogs learn by observing our behavior? Using verbal cues is convenient, but we also happen to be using those words all the time as well.

For instance, you may ask your friend to sit down and have a drink, and suddenly, your dog in the other room hears it and sits down.

So, **words alone are only one piece of the puzzle**. The other cue is body language. Going back to that "sit" command, I look at the pup in the eyes to indicate that I am talking to them and use two cues: the word "sit" or "down" (verbal) and pointing my finger down (physical). I said it loudly and firmly and used the same gesture every time.

Consistency here also means that you must always reward the desired behavior and not reward undesired behavior.

Why Positive Reinforcement Works

One reason why positive reinforcement is so powerful is that **it focuses more on the positive than the negative**. You are encouraging and rewarding your dog for desired behavior instead of punishing your dog for undesired behavior.

For one, it is **pain-free** for your dog. You are not using any kind of punishment if your dog if they display unwanted behavior. They just do not get any treat or attention. So, no yelling, violence, or anything harsh for the pup that may traumatize them, hurt your connection, and, at worst, may make them unwilling to listen to your commands

On the flip side, your dog is going to love you even more because of all the treats and toys you are giving them. They do what you want, and you give them what they want. It is a win-win.

A Warning

I must point out that **positive reinforcement is a double-edged sword**. The problem is that we do not fully understand what counts as a "reward" for dogs. Yes, treats and toys are obvious suspects, but something little as your attention can also count in certain contexts.

So, in addition to maintaining consistency in your cues, you also need to maintain discipline when handing out rewards. If your dog is doing something you don't like, do not give it any reward, even your attention.

For instance, if your dog barks at a noise in the neighborhood and you let them out every single time, guess what happens? Your dog starts to associate the reward (access to the yard) with their barking. So they will bark the next time they want to go to the yard.

Or, let's say that you want to discourage your dog from digging up the yard, so you yell and rush to them whenever they do it. They might associate your attention (the reward) with digging (the action).

As you can see, positive reinforcement can backfire, so use the reward system sparingly.

Types of Rewards

This brings us to the things you use to reward your dog. They include treats, praise, petting, toys, or games. **Food is the best motivator because every dog loves food**. In fact, it is the most efficient thing to use to get dogs to learn a behavior quickly. Other than that, here are a few more things to consider:

- The treat should be enticing and irresistible to your pet. You might need to shop around to find your dog's favorite treat.
- Size matters. The treat should be small, about the size of a pea, or smaller if you have a smaller dog. It should also be soft so your dog can eat it in a second and look to you for more. Do not give anything they need to chew or something that crumbles into bits on the floor.
- Variety is the spice of life. Have some treats nearby, so your dog does not get bored of getting the same stuff every time.
- The first thing a dog should learn is when they did something right. Praise them by saying "yes" or "good boy" in a happy voice and give them the treat.

If your dog is not as motivated by food, which is a rare occurrence (and a good reason to see the vet), petting, toys, or a short play can also be effective.

Also, the reward has to be pleasant for your dog. For instance, some dog trainers use dog collars and try to justify that when the electric shock stops, it is a reward for the dog.

It is not. Relief is not a reward.

Shock training is cruel for many reasons. For one, your dog is not going to know what you want them to do in the first place. So, they may get shocked 10, 20, or 50 times. They may learn what they should not do, yes, but they do not learn what they should do. Plus, they get nothing when they perform the right action, nothing other than a reprieve from the pain. So, shock training is ineffective and painful.

Positive reinforcement is far more effective because your dog knows quickly what they should do. Yes, they will not get it right the first ten times or so, but they do not suffer for their mistakes. Plus, they pick up what they need to do quickly because you reinforce it with treats.

What if your dog is on a special diet? Food rewards are still effective, but you need to alter your strategy. Using a canned version of the special kibble you feed your dog is an excellent alternative. However, when spoon-feeding your dog, make sure they do not eat the entire spoon. They could use some practice licking it, or you can just use a food tube.

Alternatively, you can use something that is an ingredient in your dog's special diet, such as chicken, fish, etc. You can also make treats at home and tailor the ingredients to suit your dog. There are countless recipes out there, so give it a shot!

When to Give Treats

When your dog is starting to learn a new behavior, you need to reward them every single time they demonstrate that behavior. You need that continuous reinforcement to ensure that the behavior sticks and becomes a habit.

Does that mean you will go through packs of treats every week? Only for the first week or so. Once your dog has reliably learned the behavior, you can then wean them off the treat and switch to intermittent reinforcement. Here's how I did it:

- After the dog learned the behavior, reward them 4 out of every 5 times they performed the behavior. Then, reduce to 3 out of 5, and so on. Just make sure not to reduce the frequency too quickly, otherwise you might confuse the pup. Do this until you are only rewarding occasionally.
- Though the flow of treats may run dry, keep up the praising every time with petting or alternative rewards. However, after your dog has learned the behavior, your praise can sound less excited.
- Randomize the reward frequency. Keep your dog guessing when they will get their treat. If you

reward them every other time you tell them to sit down, they will only sit down every other time. They need to learn that if they keep responding the right way, they will get what they want. In this case, a treat and your praise.

With this system, you will see that you do not have to carry packs of treats with you everywhere. With time, your dog will learn to work for your verbal praise instead since they love your attention and they are guaranteed to get it every time. Plus, they will love you even more when you surprise them with a treat when they have been a good boy/girl.

But will using so many treats can cause your dog to constantly beg for food? It really depends on the context and how you treat your dog. For example, if you feed your dog from the dinner table, chances are that they will stick around for some extra handouts. However, if you use treats only during training sessions, your dog knows that they are working and there are rewards at the end of it.

Another thing to note is that **praises alone are not enough**. Keep in mind that dogs do not really understand what we are saying. "Good boy" sounds like praise to you, but to a dog, it means that a treat may be coming their way. So, praises mean nothing to your dog. They have to be accompanied by rewards like treats, toys, petting, etc.

Shaping Behavior

Certain behaviors are complex, and it can be difficult for your dog to pick up precisely what they need to do. In such a case, you might need to use a technique called "shaping," which involves reinforcing a behavior that is close to the desired behavior and then slowly and gradually requiring your dog to do more to get a treat.

For instance, if you want to teach your dog to "shake," it can be too much to expect your dog to lift their paw off the ground and put it on your hand. So, we can teach them in several parts like so:

- Lifting a paw off the ground
- Lifting it higher
- Putting it on your hand
- Letting you hold their paw
- Pinning the "shake" command

And through these 5 parts, reward your dog every time they successfully perform the desired behavior.

When to Stop

You don't unless you want your dog to stop learning that behavior. If you want your dog to keep doing that behavior, you need to keep rewarding it. Remember that your dog performs the desired behavior not because you say the magic word but because they know that if you say the word and they do the behavior, they will get the reward. In short, they follow your command because of the reward, not because you say so.

Key Takeaways

- Positive reinforcement uses rewards to encourage good behavior
- It is effective because it is quick, pleasant and pain-free for your dog
- Food is the most powerful motivator, making treats the most efficient reward for positive reinforcement
- Cues and timing are everything. Make sure you give your dog clear verbal and physical cues and reward them immediately when they perform the action.
- Positive reinforcement can backfire and lead to undesirable habits, so understand what the reward is in different contexts to curb bad behaviors.

The next chapter is where the fun begins. Your work as a dog owner starts even before your dog gets home, and we will cover exactly what you need to do to create the best environment for your pup.

Chapter 3: Prep Works

"Money can buy you a fine dog, but only love can make him wag his tail." – Kinky Friedman

Your responsibility as a dog owner starts when you decide to get a dog. Having an ideal environment for your dog can set it up for life. I will tell you what you need to consider and do to create just that.

Responsibilities

While a dog is a great companion, you need to remember that they also require a fair bit of maintenance. While food, water, and shelter are enough to keep a dog alive, **a happy dog needs much more**.

Some owners are not ready for the responsibilities ahead of them, and I have worked with a few adopted dogs whose previous owners gave up because they "misbehaved" or because they were no longer cute. You are not ready to get a dog if you only want a puppy and do not want to take on the responsibility of raising an adult dog.

So, before anything else, consider whether now is a good time in your life to have a dog. Chances are that you will be spending anywhere between 10 to 15 years with a dog, if not more. If yes, ask yourself the following questions:

- Does everyone else in the household want a dog?
- Do I have time to provide adequate exercises and attention for my dog, in both rain and shine?
- Do I have time to give my dog the training and socialization they need?
- Can I afford the medication bills such as vaccinations?
- Can I provide my dog with a safe and secure home for the rest of its life?

Dog Breeds

There are countless of them, and they all behave differently. For instance, a herding breed will have a different temperament from a guarding or toy breed. It would take us forever to go through each one of them, so how can you determine which one works for you?

Ask your friends and colleagues about their dogs and see if you like any of them. From there, you can do a bit of online research to narrow down your options.

I recommend taking as much time as you need here because this is a major commitment, so **you want to make the right choice**. Learn everything you can about their temperaments and needs, then make a list of potential breeds that may be suitable, and pick one based on how compatible it is with your personality, lifestyle, and other personal preferences

Although, if you would allow me, **I highly encourage you to adopt rather than buy**. The dog breeding industry is not that ethical, to put it lightly. Rather than fueling that cycle, you can give unfortunate pups a second chance at life. **This little act of kindness will not change the world, but you will change their world**.

Of course, you may not have that many options if you want to adopt dogs. Some shelters may be dedicated to specific breeds, but that is very rare. Chances are that you will get crossbred dogs.

In that case, you are going it rather blind. It will be challenging to determine their temperaments and characteristics. In that case, you can ask the shelter staff what the dog is like and see if you can learn more about their parents' breeds if that is possible.

Time to Pick

When you are satisfied with your research and gathered all the information you can, it is time to make a decision. I have here another list of questions to help you make a better decision:

- Do I fully understand the dog's history and preferences?
- Have I taken the dog out for a "test run" either by going for a walk or having a short play session, so I understand what they are really like away from the kennels?
- Do I have a full veterinary history? What past operations and illnesses does the dog have? What about vaccinations?
- What help do I have access to if there are veterinary or behavioral problems after I have adopted the dog?

If you buy a dog, make sure you secure a written agreement that taking them is subject to a satisfactory veterinary inspection within 72 hours of you doing so. If you adopt one, check if there is pet insurance that covers any earlier, unforeseen veterinary costs.

Other Things to Consider

- Veterinary treatment can get expensive quickly, so make sure you are covered with pet insurance. Speak to the vet to help you decide which one is the best.
- Some countries have requirements for your dog such as having a microchip, or a collar with your name and address when it is out in public. Understand your country's law about dogs before you get one.
- Different breeds require a different amount of exercise, but they all need a good walk every day.

Preparing for Arrival

With all the above information, you should know exactly which dog to get. That is only half of the work. The other half is what you can do to create a welcoming environment for the pup.

The Groundwork

- Think about the dog's schedule for feeding, playing, training, walking, and potty time. If other people are living with you, consider delegating responsibilities. Decide who is responsible for what.
- Dog-proof your home by finding and removing hazardous items. If it is a choking hazard for children, it is also for dogs. Also, put away valuable

items that your dogs could chew or swallow.
- Get all the supplies for your dog, such as a leash, collar, ID tag, crate or gate, bed, bowls, treat, toys, grooming supplies, waste bags, etc.
- Decide where your dog will eat and sleep and where the supplies are stored. Everyone in the house should know this.

Scheduling

For humans, a life of routine, though predictable and comfortable, is boring. Dogs love routines, and they are happiest and most comfortable when they can consistently stick with one. While they can decide what they want to do throughout the day, it is just better if you help put together a schedule to get all their needs met.

Plus, if left to their own device, **dogs may learn unwanted behavior that can be difficult to stop**. Then again, we all tend to pick up bad habits if we don't keep ourselves busy, right?

You should have precise feeding, exercise, and potty time. Make sure everyone in the house is involved in this process because everyone is responsible for the dog.

In addition to making dog care simpler for humans, dogs also love a precise schedule because they know what to expect at a certain time. While it creates a dulling sense of monotony for humans, it is security and comfort for your dog.

An added benefit of scheduling here is that it also

improves the training efficiency of your dog. They know that it is time to learn, so they pay more attention to you rather than goofing off.

I will break down the scheduling for each activity below.

Food

Feed your dog precisely in terms of:

- How much to feed
- When the dog eats
- Where the dog eats
- How the food is provided

Consult your vet about what food you should be feeding your dog and how much based on their size, age, breed, health, and activity level. **2 meals a day, at most 12 hours apart, is the minimum**. 3 smaller meals also work.

The package of the dog food should give you clear feeding instructions. Make sure to check and top off the water bowl at all times.

When it comes to location, it should be far from foot traffic. You don't want to step on your dog's bowl.

Consider taking your dog out to expel right after mealtime as well because you want to get on top of potty training as soon as possible, so you want to figure out when they need to go just as quickly. Speaking of which...

Potty

Think ahead. Your dog should be let outside at the first sign that they need to dispel. One telltale sign is that your dog starts to scratch at or circle the door and whine. Don't wait and let them out, preferably with a leash on in the beginning.

Here, I want you to monitor when your dog expels. Keep a spreadsheet if needed. If you keep the feeding and drinking time precise, then your dog should also have a predictable potty time.

The goal is not about controlling when they go do their #1s and #2s (that comes later), but rather to capitalize on the opportunity to potty train them (more on that later). When they know where they need to expel, they will just go straight to their litter box or the backyard to do their business without you keeping an eye on them.

And you will need to keep an eye on your dog in the early phase of their potty training in case they run off somewhere and cause an accident.

Exercise and Play

Dogs have a certain amount of energy every day that they need to expend. Whether it is on productive or destructive behavior depends on how you schedule exercise and play.

Exercise is obviously the most important thing for your dog's health. Tire your dog through productive exercising, and they will not have the energy to pursue destructive behaviors. Neglect can lead to weight problems due to the inadequate amount of movement and the way lethargy can affect your dog's mood and hormones

The most effective exercise is walking. Take your dog outside for some walks. Both you and the dog need the walk, anyway. Plus, it creates an opportunity for your dog to socialize with other humans and animals, not to mention that you strengthen the bond with your dog when you do something together.

Walks should be kept to 5-10 minutes before you learn how your dog reacts to different stimuli.

An alternative form of enrichment is playing with toys. They keep your dog busy until it is time for a walk. A chew toy is a good alternative to your shoes, and other interactive toys can provide enough mental stimulation that they do not need to go digging in the backyard.

Training

When it comes to training, you need to keep everything short and interesting. Since dogs have a short attention span, there is no point in having long training sessions. By the time you are done, your dog will have forgotten what you taught it 5 minutes ago.

I split my training sessions into several bouts per day. Instead of working on a single dog for 15 minutes, I change it to 3 5-minute sessions. I also end the training on a good note, usually with play or a walk outside. That way, you program your dog to look forward to the next class.

Pro tip: Consider putting the training sessions right before mealtime. By then, your dog is probably already hungry so treats are even more effective.

Key Takeaways

- Make sure you are ready to raise a dog. It is a decade-long commitment, if not more, and you can't back out after a few weeks.
- Make sure you pick the right dog based oitsir temperament and needs. Ask around and do your own research.
- Have a pet insurance
- Have a precise schedule for your dog
- Feed your dog regularly. 2-3 meals a day, 12 hours apart at most.
- Keep a close eye on when your dog does their business. It'll help a lot when you potty train them.
- Keep your dog busy so they don't have time for bad habits
- Keep training short.

With all the groundwork done, you are now ready to welcome your dog into your home. In the next chapter, we will go over what you must do on the first day and the fundamental skills your dog needs to learn.

Chapter 4: Week One

"The dog lives for the day, the hour, even the moment." – Robert Falcon Scott

With all that said and done, it is time to go get your dog and introduce them to its new and forever home. In this chapter, we will focus on 5: their first day, hand-feeding, crate training, potty training, and introduction to the leash. All of this essential skill training should be done simultaneously as opportunities allow it. Let's begin!

The First Day

You want to start this beautiful relationship off on the right foot. You should have the schedule ready, so it is just a matter of following it from the second day forward. Here are some things to consider:

- Travel: Though possible to do it alone, **it is best to have another person with you**. Think of where the dog will sit after you pick them up. One person drives, and another keeps an eye on the dog. Have some towels handy in case your dog has motion sickness on the way home.
- Be direct: The only errand you need to run for the trip is to pick up the dog itself. Do not do anything else along the way. **Get the dog home as soon**

as possible. You can do some other things after the dog is safe at home.

- Keep it low-key: Although having a new member in the family is cause for celebration, do not throw parties. Your pup may become overwhelmed or over-excited. If you must, limit visitors for the first few days. Your pup needs time to adjust to its new home in peace.
- Let the pup roam: Your dog will become curious about its new environment and want to look around. Let them familiarize themselves with their surroundings. Here, you will see that they do a lot of sniffing around. You can let them explore the yard and the outdoor area around your home as well, but make sure to keep them on a leash.
- Introduction: If you live with others, it is also an excellent time to introduce them to your dog. The way I like to do this is to have people wait in a separate area and bring them in one by one. Then, I let the dog approach each person on its own – let them lead the interaction. I find that giving each person some treats to give to the pup is effective as well since the dog will associate everyone in the house with pleasant things. **During the initial interaction, do not hug, kiss, pick up, stare at, or pat the top of the head**. It can be unnerving for the dog at first. You can do that later once the dog is familiar with everyone.
- Stay close: When it is time for exercise, do not take

them out for long walks outside. Stay close to your home for now. The best place would be somewhere familiar but also quiet.

- If you have other dog(s): Also introduce them in the same fashion, but keep a leash on both dogs, loose but ready in case things go south. Never leave them alone together until you are certain nothing terrible will happen. They should also meet in a food and toy-free zone.
- If you have other cat(s): Similar to above, monitor the interaction and keep the cat safe. Other than the disapproving look that your cat may give you (let's face it, cats are like that), young pups should have no trouble interacting with cats. The cat might give your pup a few taps, but that is about it. Older dogs, however, may be problematic, so be careful.
- Give your dog time: It is their first day, so everything is strange to them. **Allow them the time and quiet to explore and just get comfortable with their new home.** There will be time for play later. Although, at the end of the day, designate a room where your dog will stay for the next couple of weeks. It's important to keep them in a single place for crate training and potty training.

Hand-Feeding

Although your dog will get to eat from their food bowl, the goal of this training is to send a message to your dog.

It is your food they are eating and you are the source of every good thing a dog could want: food, water, shelter, toys, and play. You want your dog to see you as a benevolent, higher-ranking being and that they should respect you.

Another benefit to hand-feeding is that you stop your dog from guarding its food because you introduce safety. It is natural for dogs to guard their food jealously, which can be dangerous and unpredictable. So, this practice helps mellow out your dog.

Here's how to do it.

Step 1: Small Bites

Start by putting a bit of dog food into the bowl. Then, take some from the bowl in your hand and let your leashed dog eat out of it. Do this for the whole meal, for every meal, for the whole week.

This requires you to put small amounts of food into the bowl, scoop small amounts of it into your hands, feed your dog, and then refill the bowl until the dog is sufficiently fed.

Use your bare hands. No gloves, and certainly do not be squeamish. Think of it as finger painting. Make sure to wash your hand before and after every feeding session. Make sure that you get all the soap off before feeding.

When your dog is eating from your hand, it is a good

opportunity to teach them their name. Say their name softly in a loving way. Do it whenever you hand-feed your dog.

Step 2: Touching

As the week progresses and your dog starts to be more comfortable eating from your hand, try touching their collar or pet on the side of their body and see how they react.

If your dog stops eating, stop touching them and continue to offer them food. You can also try switching which hand you are feeding them with.

When your dog starts to be more comfortable being touched when eating, try touching a bit between each bowl refill. Make sure that your dog sees you refilling the bowl before you continue feeding them.

Also, between handfuls of dog food, make sure your dog looks at you before you give them more food. If they don't, wait a bit, and they should. Again, the goal is to get the dog to see you as their source of food.

Step 3: Bowl Feeding

Next is to try to let your dog eat from the bowl that you hold in your lap. If your dog is hesitant, try holding it further forward and slowly bringing it in.

You know you have succeeded when your dog is comfortable with eating from the bowl you hold close to your body without rearing away from you when you touch them.

Step 4: Switching Things Up

As the week progresses, get your dog used to eating in different ways. Try changing your feeding hand, using different containers to store the dog food, feeding your dog in different rooms, especially in the car.

Again, try touching your dog's collar or side. The goal is to get your dog comfortable with being touched in different situations.

You will need to touch your dog's collar a lot throughout the training over the next 4 weeks. It makes handling the dog easier. You might need to control your dog in a few seconds, other people can check the collar for your information if needed, and the vets and groomers will thank you for the training.

Crate Training

An essential skill that every good boy should know. If done properly, the crate should not be a place of confinement and isolation. Instead, **it is a place of security and stability**. The crate is also a powerful tool to help you establish rules and order in your home.

There are many reasons why this is the highest priority:

- House training: The goal is that you want your dog to treat their crate the same way a wild dog would

their den, or you would your bedroom – you do not expel where you sleep. You define where the dog sleeps, which also helps define where they can do their business. Also, you will know that your dog needs to do it first thing when you let them out of the crate in the morning.
- Transport: When your dog is familiar with the crate early on, getting them in there is easy. They will not bark, whine, or struggle inside the crate. Win-win for both you and the dog.
- Boundary: Your dog will also learn that the house is your territory. They need to learn early on what they can and cannot do. When you put them in a crate when you are occupied, you limit their access to the rest of the house so they cannot misbehave. When you let them out, it will be when you are there to reinforce or dissuade certain behaviors. So, your dog learns that the crate is their personal space and the rest of the house is your kingdom.

You also need to pick the right crate for the job. You need to think about size and material.

Picking the size is easy. It is too small if your dog cannot stand up and turn around while in it. But do not get one so large that your dog is comfortable with doing its business in one corner and sleeping in another.

Materials are trickier, but I recommend that you get two crates.

A metal wire crate should be used in your home because

it is easy to clean, highly visible, and has adequate ventilation. Get one with a movable divider to adjust the size as your pup grows up.

A plastic crate does not allow for size adjustment, so you need to buy more in the future. But the benefit of plastic crates is that they offer more privacy, which is something your dog needs when you take them outside. They provide less visibility and ventilation, but not to the point of suffocation.

Training Process

With all of that out of the way, we can now move on to the training itself. I will break it down for you.

Step 1: Introduction

Put the crate down where there is a lot of foot traffic, like the living room. Try to touch up the crate to make it look safe and comfortable. I recommend putting a soft blanket or towel in there. If possible, have a comfortable bed for your dog inside.

Remove or open the door and let your dog explore the crate at their own pace. Some will go straight in, but others might need a bit of encouragement. If so, do the following:

- Bring your dog close to the crate and talk to your dog in a positive tone. Do not put them inside. You want to make sure that the dog knows the crate is there.

- Lure your dog by dropping treats around the crate first and then just inside the door before throwing more into the deep end. Your dog should follow the treat and go into the crate. If not, be patient and repeat the previous step until your dog voluntarily enters the crate to get the food. Sometimes, they need to be convinced with toys instead.
- Remember that it can take several days before your dog is comfortable with the crate, so be patient and give them time.

Step 2: Feeding

When your dog is starting to be more familiar with the crate, you need to start to teach your dog that its crate is its den. So, feed him near the crate first to establish a pleasant association with the crate.

- If your dog can enter the crate calmly, you can put the food dish at the back and let them enjoy their meal in peace.
- If not, see how far they are willing to go in and put the food dish there. In the following feeding sessions, move the dish a bit further into the crate until you reach the deepest end. Keep the door open for now.
- When your dog is comfortable eating in their crate, try closing the door while they are eating but open it as soon as your dog is done eating.
- From there, leave the door closed for a bit longer. Work from 1, 2, 5, and then 10 minutes.

- If your dog starts to whine to be let out, you are going too fast. Decrease the time the door stays closed next time.
- Do not open the crate immediately when they whine because they will think that you will let them out when they whine. Only let them out when they stop whining.

Step 3: Extend Crate Time

Next is to keep your dog inside the crate for longer. Do the following:

- Entice your dog into going into the crate using treats. When they go inside, pin a command such as "crate", "den", or "inside" and close the door.
- Sit close to the crate for 10 minutes, giving them a few treats for being patient, then go into another room for 5 minutes. Come back and repeat. Then, let your dog out and give them some more praise.
- In subsequent sessions, see if your dog goes inside in response to your command. Just open the door and say the command while holding a few treats in your hand. Make sure to let your dog sniff the treats first. Also, stay in the other room for longer. I work in 5-minute increments until I get to 30 minutes.
- This step can take several days or even weeks. But hey, another reason to start early, right?

Step 4: Crating When Going Outside

When your dog is comfortable staying inside the crate for 30 minutes, you can leave them in there for a short time when you leave the house. Do the following:

- Entice your dog to go into the crate using treats. Put some toys to keep them company. Give them praise and a treat when they are in.
- Leave the house anywhere from 5 to 20 minutes after they are in the crate.
- Keep your departure low-key, calm, and concise. Praise your dog for entering the crate, give them a treat for entering, close the door, and then leave (after waiting for 5-20mns).
- Keep your arrival low-key and calm as well. Your dog may get excited when they see you, so do not reward them by reflecting their excitement.
- To prevent an association between crating and being left alone, consider repeating step 3 for short periods of time now and again when you have the time.

Step 5: Crating at Night

From there, you can leave your dog in the crate overnight. Still, for the first few days, put the crate close to your bed or at least as close as possible to strengthen your bond. Also, put a water dispenser or bowl in there to keep your pup hydrated.

Move the crate further to where you want them to sleep every couple of days. Still, the final location should still be close so that you can hear your dog when they need a late-night visit to the toilet.

Caution

On top of all this, I have a few handy tips to help you successfully crate-train your pupper.

Whining

As you might have guessed, when your dog starts whining at night, you don't know whether they want to be let out or if they need to expel. If you follow the previous steps properly, then one of two things can happen.

- If the whining stops, then it was just a test to see if you would cave into their demands.
- If the whining continues for several minutes, then they really need to go expel. Open the door, take the dog out or wherever they can eliminate, wait, and bring them back into the crate after they are done. Keep the excursion brief and calm, no matter how excited your dog may be.
- Pro tip: If your dog looks into your eyes when they are "doing the business," that means they look to you for protection and to give them a heads-up if there is any danger. Your dog is vulnerable at that moment, so they want you to watch their back. I would return their glance and just stay with them until they are done.

Separation Anxiety

Unfortunately, crate training will not work if your dog has separation anxiety. They will hurt themselves trying to tear the crate open to get to you. Instead, consult a professional animal behavior specialist.

Other Things to Avoid

- Do not rush it. Let your dog settle into their crate at their own pace.
- Do not use a harsh voice or pound on the crate when your dog is whining.
- Do not use the crate to punish your dog. It is a safe haven, so keep it that way. Use it to manage behaviors instead. For instance, if you don't want any mishaps when guests are coming over, crate them during the visit rather than waiting for your dog to mess up and then punish them by crating them.
- Do not leave pups younger than 6 months old any longer than 3 hours in the crate. Their small bladder will not hold.
- Do not keep the door closed. It should only be closed when you want to keep your dog penned for a while. Outside of that, leave the door open so your dog can go in for some quiet time. Respect their needs and make sure no one disturbs the dog when they are resting inside the crate.

Potty Training

Another important thing to get out of the way early you need to make sure your dog knows where to do their #1s and #2s. This can also take a while, but that is why we want to knock it out fast.

Experts suggest potty training your dog when they are anywhere from 12 to 16 weeks old. At that point, they can control their bladder and bowel movements well enough to stay inside the crate overnight.

Potty Training Steps

If you follow the crate training process, then you are already one step ahead. The first step is to get them to hold it in. Dogs assume they can just do their business whenever and wherever they want, except where they sleep. Then, do the following:

- Think of where your dog will do their business and take them to the same spot whenever they need to. After the first session, their scent will prompt them to do their business at the same place again next time.
- Take them out to do this first thing in the morning, then once every 30 minutes to an hour, after meals, after your dog wakes up, and before they go to sleep at night.
- Pin a command when you arrive at the spot, and they start to do their thing. I use "go peeps" or

"potty" in a calm voice. After they are done, give them a praise and a treat.

- Stay with your dog the entire time.
- Keep their eating schedule regular and precise. Take away their food between meals.
- Note down when your dog does their business. I write "1" for peeing and "2" for pooping.

Potty Training Tips

- Learn the sign: Dogs show visible signs when they need to go such as smelling their rear, pacing in circles, barking or scratching at the door that leads to their potty spot, sniffing the floor, etc.
- Have a leash at the door so you can put it on and get your dog out at a moment's notice.
- Handling accidents: Do not punish your dog. If you catch them in the act, quickly clean up their mess and lead or take her to the potty area.
- Make sure to clean the area of the accident thoroughly. Any leftover scent will prompt your dog to go at the same spot next time.
- Do not give your dog free access to the entire house until they are potty trained.
- Use a litter box if you live in an apartment.
- A full bladder is an unstoppable force. When your dog needs to go, even in bad weather, take them to their spot. Have an umbrella ready if it frequently rains in your area. Shovel around the spot if it snows to create a familiar sight.

- Keep an eye on your pup. If you are busy, confine them to a room or their crate. Keep them in an area small enough that they do not want to eliminate there.
- The rule of thumb is that a pup can hold one hour for every month of age. So, a 2-month-old pup can hold for 2 hours. Confining them for any longer than that, and you risk having an accident.

Introducing the Leash

When it comes to leashing, the goal is to accomplish the following:

- Get your dog comfortable with having a collar and leash on
- Feeling more connected to you
- Teaching them about boundaries
- Getting them to read your body language

You have two options when leashing your dog. You can just hold onto the leash or hook it to your belt or somewhere that frees up both your hands as needed.

When it comes to the leash, make sure you get a leash at least 6-foot long. Think of where your dog would be walking in relation to you as well. If your dog walks on your right, hold the handle with your left and the middle of the leash with your right, with the leash crossing in front of you. Switch hands if you prefer the left. **Also, have lots of treats ready.**

Here's how to do it.

Step 1: Trail Leashing

Some dogs do not like it when they are leashed or tethered. So, start slow by leashing them for 5 seconds first and see how they react. Give them a treat from the same hand if they remain calm. Work your way up from there.

Step 2: Walking on the Leash

The next step is to allow your dog to roam around while still being tethered to you. That means whenever you let your dog out of their room, leash them and supervise their behavior. For now, train in the room your dog is confined to.

Your dog may want to run off somewhere, but through tethering, you are teaching them that so long as the leash is on, you determine how far your dog can go and what they can and cannot do. You want your dog to learn about you and understand that you are in control.

In this step, walk around your house or the backyard with the dog tethered to you. But when your dog starts to pull, stop and stand your ground. You only walk (and consequently, your dog can only walk) when the leash is loose. Say "good" and continue walking.

When your dog is leashed to you, let other family members or friends come to your dog and give them a treat before having them back up.

You know you have succeeded when your dog is comfortable with being leashed. They should be calm when leashed and always follow you where you go. At that point, you can allow them free roam (make sure they are crate-trained and potty-trained first, though!).

Potential Problems

- Chewing: If your dog chews on the leash, soak the leash in unsweetened mouthwash or spray it with a bitter apple.
- Jumping: If your dog jumps on you when you approach, leash them to a table leg or doorknob, then back up and approach slowly. If your dog jumps, walk away for a moment before trying again. Your dog will eventually learn that they are not supposed to jump on you, and you can leash them to your belt again.

Key Takeaways

For your first week, the goal is to get your pup settled into its new home.

- Allow your dog to look around your house with your supervision before limiting their access until they are properly trained
- Keep everything calm so as not to overstimulate the poor pup

- For the first week, hand-feed your dog by pouring the dog food into the bowl and using your hand to feed it directly to your dog
    - The idea is to get your dog comfortable with you handling them while they are eating as well as their bowl to curb food guarding
    - Wash your hand before and after every feeding session
- For crate training, get your dog to familiarize themselves with the crate first
    - Introduce your dog to it and try to get them to go inside by making the space comfortable and letting them eat while inside
    - Do not keep your pup in there for too long, lest they soil themselves and the crate. The general rule is that a puppy can hold it in for 1 hour longer for every month of age
    - Still, keep a close eye on your pup and let them out if they show signs that they need to go do their business
    - Do not let them out when they whine or scratch
- Potty training is best done in conjunction with crate training
    - Your dog should have a predictable schedule if you feed them at regular times
    - Take note when they urinate and defecate to help you understand the pattern

    - Do not punish your dog if they accidentally do it in your home. Take them outside as soon as possible so they can finish their business and clean up the mess
    - Make sure to take your dog to the same spot every time
    - Keep an eye out for signs that your dog needs to go. Pacing, whining, and scratching the door are common signs
- Start leash training by tethering your dog to you. They will try to pull, but you need to stand firm. Teach them that you decide where to go, not the dog.

Next week, we will work on basic skills a dog should know, such as sitting, down, and leash walking.

Chapter 5: Week Two

"The dog lives for the day, the hour, even the moment." – Robert Falcon Scott

The first week is all about basic but fundamental skills. These take a long time, but at the end of the first week, your dog should have a good grasp of the aforementioned skills.

I should also mention that if your dog is not proficient at the skills highlighted in the first week, that is totally okay. Some dogs take longer to train than others. Just keep at it in the second week as well. Potty training is the most difficult skill to teach, which you will need to continue teaching well beyond this 4-week program.

In the second week, it is time to teach them all the basic commands in the second week. But first, let's talk about one of the most important developmental milestones for your dog: socialization.

Socialization

Many dogs in shelters or rescue organizations are not well socialized. **People like to think that it is the dog's fault, but I believe the blame lies with the owner.**

Dogs should get plenty of socialization with other people and animals early on. It helps both the dog and you in the long run when they are well-socialized.

Consider setting up playgroups with people who also own dogs. If not, you can ask the vet or groomer if they know anyone you can contact who has well-behaved dogs.

To make socialization easier for your dog, consider starting with similarly sized dogs to take away that intimidation factor. This is especially important if you have very small puppies.

Taking your dog to a dog care center is also a good idea. Your dog will get plenty of socialization with other dogs and humans while you are away. Plus, the professionals there will help reinforce any good behaviors and curb bad ones in your absence.

Eye Contact

The first and most important skill your dog needs to learn is how to focus. In this case, they need to learn that they need to look at you. It is indeed a simple and easy skill to learn and master, but **it is fundamental to teaching them other skills down the line**, even those beyond the scope of this book.

Before you begin, make sure that the training area has no sources of distractions, be it toys or other dogs. If you have small dogs, you might need to sit down first to be closer to them. Do the following:

- First, hold a treat close to your dog's nose. Let them have a whiff.
- Say something like "Focus" a few times while pulling back the treat
- Your dog's eyes should be locked to the treat now, so slowly bring it between your eyes
- Maintain direct eye contact with your dog
- Go for 2 seconds of eye contact for now and reward your dog by bringing the treat from your eyes to their mouth
- Later on, try increasing the duration of the eye contact, and then use your finger instead of a treat

Focus Up

You will be burning through a lot of treats if you haven't already. This is why you should train your dog right before mealtime. Hunger enhances the effectiveness of treats even further.

For this training, treats are used to direct your dog's attention, but the final goal is to get your dog to follow your hand movement. More specifically, your hand will guide them to perform different actions. Through repetitions, your dog will soon learn to follow your fingertips, and training will be far easier down the line.

Remember the hand-feeding training from last week? If you follow it closely, your dog should look at your hand fondly. **They should already understand that treats and other goodies come from your hand.**

So, here's how to do it.

Step 1: Presentation

First, hold a treat at your fingertip. Bring it slowly to your dog's nose and let them have a whiff. Then, move it around slowly and observe how your dog's gaze also follows your hand.

Step 2: Taste Test

Say your dog's name to help them remember and praise them. Bring the treat in so they can nibble at it, but not too much. During that time, try touching the dog's collar and its side. They should not jump or rear away anymore.

Before your dog has too much treat, slowly move your hand away, so your dog follows your hand again. At this point, your dog may become distracted or lose interest.

If so, move the treat closer again to try and grab their attention. Also, try saying their name in a happy voice and be overall energetic, so your dog pays attention to you.

Step 3: Switching Things Up

Then, try moving your hand to a different area or vary the speed of the movement.

The entire exercise should last no longer than a few minutes. When done, let your dog eat the treat from your hand after you praise and touch their side and collar.

Sit

This command is more versatile than you think. **It is the foundation of other commands such as "down," "stay," etc.** You can also use it to reinforce other good behaviors.

For instance, when you are taking your dog out for walks, you can give them a command to sit before you open the door. That way, your dog would not dart right out the moment the door swings clear.

Or maybe you want to reinforce good table manners. You can order your dog to sit before they get their meal (more on that in Week 4), instead of jumping and clawing at you when you bring out the dog food or to sit patiently while you have dinner.

So, this is how you teach your dog to sit.

- Start by holding a lure in your hand and let your dog have a whiff.
- Slowly raise it above your dog's head. Their eyes should be glued to the treat, and they would try to get their nose as close to the treat as possible.
- When you get the treat high enough, your dog will sit down so they can lift their head higher.
- The moment your dog's rear touches the floor, say "good" or "good boy/girl" and feed them.
- While they are enjoying their reward, pet them around the collar.

- Give them pets and praises for about 5 seconds, and your dog needs to be focused on you. Show a bit more excitement and energy if you need to.

From there, it is a matter of repetition. It will take at least 10 attempts before your dog learns that they need to sit to get a treat. You need to do this a lot more often throughout the week, maybe even into the third and fourth week to really drive in that lesson.

You might also notice that I never mentioned saying the command itself. The idea is to get your dog to understand what they need to do first. They need to think that they may get a treat if they sit.

Once your dog understands and sits without much effort from you, then you can attach a command by saying "sit" before you direct them to sit down. Then, just rinse and repeat throughout multiple sessions until your dog understand that you want them to sit down when you say "sit." From there, you can also add a hand signal in addition to the verbal command. I prefer pointing down, but you can also raise your palm.

Pro tip: Do not push down your dog's rear to get them to sit. It teaches them nothing. If anything, it teaches them to give up and let you physically manipulate them instead, which is not what we want.

Down

Down is a natural progression after “sit,” so it makes sense to teach this after your dog has mastered “sit.” Just like humans, dogs are more willing to lie down if they are on a soft surface. So, if you are not training your dog in your backyard, make sure they at least have a carpet to lie on.

Consider kneeling through this training, so your dog does not have to look up at you. Some dogs will need a bit more time to figure out this command depending on their temperament, leg length, age, etc. Follow the steps below:

- Your dog starts in a sitting position
- Take out a treat and hold it to their nose. Let them take a whiff.
- Pin a command like “Down” and slowly bring the treat to the floor
- Your dog should start to bow down to follow the treat
- At this point, they may stand up because the treat is in an uncomfortable position, which is what we want
- Try to entice your dog into a bow position – as in, head down, rear up
- If you are having trouble, try to move the treat closer or away from your dog as you bring the treat down. One of the two will work for your pup

- When your dog is in that bow position, hold the treat there until your dog becomes tired and drops their rump
- Give them the treat as soon as your dog lies down

One common problem I encounter is that **some dogs just will not go down.** One effective way to deal with this problem is by sitting on the floor with your feet flat and making the shape of an A with your knees. Then, use the treat to lure your dog under you. They have no choice but to go down to get that treat.

Leash Walking (Basic)

Dogs love going for walks. In addition to the change of scenery and loads of socializations and interactions, your dog will also get a good workout in. That said, it would not be as fun if your dog just pulls you in all directions whenever they wanted.

A good walk is controlled. The leash should be quite loose as your dog walks by your side. It must be said that even the best dogs pull on the leash sometimes, so do not be discouraged if your dog does the same. You are a very lucky person if you got a dog that does not pull at all, especially with no prior training.

The goal of this exercise is not to go on long walks. If anything, it teaches your dog how they should behave on walks as well as how to hold a leash and manage your dog's inevitable pulling. Think of this training as preparation for walking outside, which you will do next week.

For this exercise, do the following:

Step 1: Focus Up

First, you want to make sure your dog focuses on you. Look into their eyes and make sure they return it. Then, hold a treat in one hand and try to lure your dog in the direction you want to go. Slowly walk forward and give plenty of slack on the leash.

Step 2: Controlling Movement

There will be times when your dog gets too excited and try to run somewhere. In such a case, put your feet down and stand still. Hold the leash to your chest and hold it until your dog calms down.

Step 3: Reward

Reward your dog with a treat and say "good" whenever they look at you. It teaches your dog to check where you are going, so they can match pace. If your dog does not look at you, maybe you need to break down the lesson more.

Your dog will try to pull away when you walk around, so when that happens, stop. They will lean against the leash without taking a step forward. When they stop and the leash slacks, praise them.

If your dog still does not look at you, make a small sound to get their attention. If your dog still looks elsewhere, pull yourself toward the dog. Think of it as pulling a rope – one hand in front of the other. Then, use the treat to lure the dog into going in the other direction.

If your dog turns to look at you when you pull yourself in, stop. Give your dog a praise, and lure again.

Key Takeaway

- Now would be an excellent time to get your dog to socialize. That way, they can interact with people and other dogs normally when they grow up

- The first thing you want to teach your dog is to ask them to give their attention. This is important so they can pick up on cues later down the line
- The second most important skill your dog needs to learn is to follow your direction. You will use this a lot to teach your dog how to perform certain actions
- Sit is a crucial skill your dog needs to master because you can use it to instill discipline in different contexts
    - Use a treat and hold it above your dog's head, so they sit down in an attempt to reach it
    - Pin a command like "Sit"
    - Praise and reward
- Down is a great exercise to control your dog's impulse
    - Start from a sitting position and guide your dog to lie down with a treat
    - Reward when your dog's rump touches the floor
- The second step in walking your dog involves a practice run in the yard. Keep the leash slack but be ready to stand your ground and hold it tight if your dog wants to run off somewhere.

In week three, we will look at some more advanced commands, some of which can be used to stop your dog from partaking in destructive behaviors.

Chapter 6: Week Three

"Just because a dog is not giving you the response you're looking for, doesn't mean he is a hard dog." – Ivan Balabanov

Congratulations! You are already halfway there! Just like last week, your dog might not be proficient at certain skills. If that is the case, continue to work on them into the third week because your dog needs to be relatively good at it to learn the skills we cover this week. The commands you will teach your dog this week are intended to instill discipline.

Stay

This is another extension of the "sit" command. Now you see how useful it is to teach your dog to learn how to sit. You are basically asking your dog to sit in one spot for a while, which is useful in keeping your dog away from trouble.

Pro tip: Have a natural barrier that your dog must overcome if they want to move away. Try putting them on a stool or a chair, so your dog is more willing to sit there. Any elevated platform is fine – height does not matter.

Follow these steps:

- Start by having your dog sit on the stool or chair
- Show them your palm, put it about a foot from their face, and say "stay"
- Keep holding out your hand like that and then take a step back
- Take a step forward
- Go to your dog and give them a treat if they remain still the whole time

Make sure that the treat is out of sight the entire time. I put it in my back pocket or hold it behind my back in my other hand. If your dog sees the treat, they may become excited and break their stay.

Of course, you also want your dog to stay when they are sitting on flat ground, not on a chair. So, when your dog can stay more consistent, you can try to get them to stay on the floor.

One problem here is that dogs sometimes will just jump off the stool or chair. You must address this problem as soon as possible because training them to stay after they have the experience of jumping off during the stay is going to be very difficult.

If your dog jumps off the first couple of times, it is time to change tactics. **Lower your expectations and reward your dog for the small wins.** Try standing closer to your dog and having them stay for only a few seconds, and then slowly increase the distance and duration when your dog is being consistent.

Another thing I must mention is that your success depends mostly on you as well. That means, maintaining strong body posture, eye contact, and hand signal. Make sure you stand up straight and be firm. Your dog will pick up the clue and be just as serious during the training.

Come

Also known as "recall," the command tells your dog to approach you. Although this command appears to restrict or control your dog's movement, it is crucial for your dog's safety.

When your dog masters this command, it actually allows them more freedom to interact and socialize with other people and animals. The bad news is that you might need another person to help you out.

Here's how to do it:

- Have your dog remain in one spot, and have another person hold them if possible
- Give your dog a treat and take 3 steps backward
- Let the other person release the dog
- Get down on your knees and call "Come!" in an excited voice. Your dog may not understand what to do at first but keep at it.
- When your dog comes, surprise them with a treat. This is to get your dog to think that they will get one if they come to you.

Consider taking only a step or two back if your dog does not come to you. If they come to you and sit down consistently, you can try taking 5 steps or so back and see if they come to you.

Pro tip: Have a jar of treats in every room so you can reward your dog for successfully coming to you.

Drop It

This is a bit of an advanced technique, which is why it is later down the list. It also requires some basic discipline from previous tricks such as sit and stay.

Regardless, this is a crucial skill. You want your dog to let go of your shoe or dirty laundry. **This command goes a long way in stopping unwanted behavior in its tracks.**

Stopping unwanted behavior by not rewarding it is only one piece of the puzzle, after all. You need to find something to replace it. This is called positive redirection. So, instead of yelling "NO!" at the top of your lungs, do the following:

- Show your dog a treat and say "drop it"
- Repeat your command until your dog does it
- When they do, get them to sit and give them a treat

Now, you may be wondering if giving your dog a treat this way is going to reinforce bad behavior. After all, they may associate the treat with the shoe or whatever they have in their mouth at the moment and try to do the same thing next time they want treats.

This is why timing the reward is critical. Your dog may be convinced that they are rewarded if they snatch your shoe if you give them a treat immediately after they drop it.

However, you will notice that this training does not follow that sequence. Instead, you add another action between letting go of the shoe and the reward itself. Therefore, your dog is going to assume that they are being rewarded for sitting down, which is what you have been doing already ever since you taught your dog to sit.

This is not something that you can just set up a practice whenever you want, so capitalize on the opportunity to teach your dog how to drop whatever they have on command.

Leave It

Ideally, you want to be using this command before telling your dog to "drop it". **This command is used to stop your dog from snatching food or coming even close to it.**

The idea of this exercise is similar to that instant gratification experiment known as the Stanford marshmallow experiment. You can look it up a bit to understand the concept. Anyway, here is how you teach your dog to "leave it":

- Place a treat on the ground
- Naturally, your dog will try to go for it
- Say in a firm and authoritative voice to "leave it"
- Make sure to remain close to the treat because your job is to make sure they do not get to it
- Cover up the treat when they try to go for the treat
- Rinse and repeat until your dog does not move forward for 2 seconds, then say "Good" and give them a different (preferably better) treat from your pocket

At this point, you might understand why this training is toward the tail end of the 4-week program. What your dog needs to do, that is saying still, is a very simple practice that your dog should be familiar with.

However, you are asking them to go against their nature and what they understand about treats. When you first put the treat on the floor, they may think that it is an accident or some kind of mistake since you usually give them the treat directly instead of dropping it on the floor.

Regardless, a treat is a treat and they will try to go for it. When you block it, your dog will be confused. That is natural. **Give them time and be patient.** It will take them a while to figure out that they are not supposed to go for whatever it is they want when you say "leave it".

When they start to figure it out, they will have a momentary pause. That is your cue to reward their patience. Then, your dog starts to understand what they need to do through repetition.

The biggest mistake here is rewarding your dog by letting them eat the treat off the floor. Do not do that. What happens then is that you are rewarding the dog for going for the treat or desired item. You want them to ignore it.

So, the treat on the floor is only to tempt them. The actual reward is the treat you have in your hand. It also improves training efficiency to use an inferior treat as bait and your dog's favorite treat as the reward.

Leash Walking (Intermediate)

After your dog is comfortable with you handling their collar and their leash, it is time to take the training outdoors. This time, you will work on the sidewalk. The goal is to get them to stay on the sidewalk. Follow these steps:

- Leash your dog and take them outside
- Remain still first and see if your dog spots something and try to run after it
- If so, stand your ground and let the dog pull on the leash. Wait until your dog calms down and let the leash slack again
- When that happens, or if your dog remains patient by your side, say "good" and start walking
- Positioning is key: Have your dog walk on the right. As in, put yourself between your dog and the street as you walk.

- Move into the street. Your dog should start to step into it.
- Use your feet to catch their first paw that goes off the curb. Sweep it back onto the sidewalk.
- Rinse and repeat until your dog learns to sta,y on the sidewalk

Your dog should pick up this lesson in a dozen walks or so. The raised sidewalk is a clear marker to remind your dog to stay on it.

If you can, use a short leash for this training so the dog remains relatively close to you to do the paw sweep. Be delicate when you do the sweep though. You just want to move the paw back onto the sidewalk. It is just a direction, not a punishment. If you get too rough, your dog might become fearful of your feet.

Key Takeaway

- "Stay" is a test of patience
    - Have your dog sit down and take a few steps back, then one forward
    - Reward your dog if they can remain still
- Recall or "Come" helps you get your dog's attention from a distance and can be used to control interactions.
    - Take a few steps away from your dog, go down, and call your dog to come to you
    - Only show and reward them when they approach you

- "Drop it" is a crucial skill to curb bad behavior through positive redirection
    - Show your dog a treat and tell them to drop it
    - Keep at it until your dog drops whatever they have in their mouth, then ask them to sit before rewarding
    - The sequence is drop > sit > reward. That way, your dog does not think that they get rewarded for dropping the object.
- "Leave it" is also a test of patience in the face of temptation
    - Tempt your dog with a treat on the floor but block it if your dog goes for it
    - Reward your dog with a better treat if they show even a bit of restraint
- For the third stage of leash walking, take your dog outside
    - Be ready to restrain your dog if they want to dart somewhere
    - Position yourself closer to the street
    - Go off the sidewalk and try to coax your dog into following you
    - Use your feet to gently catch your dog's paw when they try to step into the street with you

For the final week of this 4-week course, your dog will learn basic manners/etiquette and other advanced commands.

Chapter 7: Week Four

"Your dog is not being a problem, your dog is having a problem."

– Chad Mackin

Finally, week four! You are nearly there now. Same thing as last time, continue to review and polish the skills your dog learned last week. This week, we will work on more complex commands and manners.

I won't lie to you. This is not going to be easy. But if you have been working closely with your dog, your dog should be quite disciplined and close to you already. In other words, it should not be too difficult to teach your dog these commands.

Sit Before Eat

After your dog is comfortable with you handling the bowl and their food, you can then let your dog eat freely from a bowl. Still, there is room for misbehavior. Your dog may get excited and jump at you when you bring out the bowl. So, you want to teach them basic manners.

In this case, you want your dog to contain themselves before meals by sitting and waiting for you to put down the bowl. So, here is what you need to do when you feed your dog:

- Put the dog food into the bowl and let your dog see it, but keep it out of their reach
- Tell your dog to sit. One of two things will happen here:
    - Your dog sits: Reward by putting the bowl down immediately
    - Your dog does not sit: Give your dog a lot of chances to sit down. You may need to lure them into a sitting position as described in Week 1.
- If your dog still does not sit, turn away and put the bowl somewhere your dog cannot reach. Wait 1 minute and try again.
- Lower your criteria for success. When your dog sits, even for a second, say "good" and then set the bowl down

This exercise teaches your dog to "ask politely" for their food instead of "demanding" it. After a couple of weeks, your dog may get so good at this that you do not even have to ask them to sit. They will just drip their rump when you bring out the bowl.

One potential problem here is that your dog may not want to sit. It could be because your dog has not understood your command yet. That said, your dog should at least be familiar with the idea of sitting down, so you can just try to lure your dog into a sitting position.

Another discipline you need to reinforce early on is that they cannot just eat whenever they want. They need to know that meal times are limited. It might take your dog a week or so to figure it out, but you need to take away the bowl after 15 minutes, whether your dog has finished their meal or not.

This also highlights the importance of hand-feeding we covered in Week 1. If you try to do this without prior training, your dog may nip your hand out of instinct.

What if you need to feed more than one dog? Do the same as above, but only feed your dogs when they all sit down. They may try to go into each other's bowls for a second helping, so you need to supervise and stand between the bowl to block that from happening.

But why wait for every dog to sit? Is it not unfair to the good dog that understands your command? It does seem a bit unfair, but you are wielding an invisible force: **peer pressure**. When you wait for other dogs to sit, the ones that are already sitting down will hint at others to do the same.

Also, if you have more than 3 dogs, make sure that the bowls are at least 6 feet from each other so you can intercept your dog when they dart for another bowl.

Off-Limits

Toward the end of the 4-week program, you may want to let your dog roam free around the house without your supervision. That is the goal, and we started by slowly introducing them to a single room and allowing access to different parts of the house as the weeks go by.

That said, no one has the time to supervise dogs all the time, so **your dog needs to understand boundaries.** You may be okay with dogs going everywhere in your home, and that is okay. This training is optional.

However, if there are certain rooms you may not want your dog to wander into, say the kitchen, then you need to teach your dog to respect boundaries.

While dogs urinate to mark their territories and boundaries, doing the same in your home is not the way to go. Instead, they need to understand that humans mark their boundaries using doors, the line between the carpet and tile, or the edge of the lawn.

Follow these steps to teach your dog this advanced discipline:

- Use your kitchen or whatever room you do not want your dog to be in as the training area
- Set up a barrier of some kind at the doorway, high enough that your dog could only poke their head over (I use a baby gate barrier)
- Give the "stay" command and walk away

- Come back immediately and give your dog a treat
- Rinse and repeat a few times before increasing the duration before you come back and reward your dog
- Switch to shorter barriers such as a board and continue increasing the duration
- At some point, your dog will hop over the barrier. When that happens, say "Out" and send your dog back to the other side. Walk them there if you have to before trying again. Only reward your dog when they learn to remain outside the boundary.

While a dog can pick up hints that the edge of the carpet is a boundary, it is difficult for them to connect the dots. I use a small 2"x2" (or 5 cm x 5 cm) board to mark boundaries. It is much more visible. Just make sure not to trip!

I also want to point out that the success of this training relies on two things: **your body language and the dog's temperament.** Maintain strong body language during the training.

As for your dog's temperament, there is not much you can do about it. Some dogs are naturally obedient, whereas others will constantly violate the rule, even if it means stepping an inch over the boundary just to see your reaction.

Still, be firm with your rules. Be consistent, and your dog will learn to obey. Remember that you need to wean your dog off the treats eventually. I recommend starting to do this a few months after your dog is disciplined enough.

Guard/Center Position

Guard dogs usually are trained to take this position by standing between your legs. It is also known as a center position. It serves many benefits.

For guard dogs, it keeps them close to their owner so they can lunge at attackers at a moment's notice. By positioning the dog so close to the owner, the attacker has no choice but to overcome the dog first.

But for an average dog owner, having your dog standing between your leg keep them close to you when you are maneuvering around a crowded area. For one, your leash won't snag on other people walking by.

Furthermore, it is a safe position for your dog to be in. No one would try and reach out to touch your dog when they are that close to you. On the flip side, it also stops your dog from licking, touching, or annoying those walking by.

So, to teach your dog this position, do the following:

- Stand up straight, feet shoulder-width apart, back turned toward your dog
- Pin a command. I say "Center" and try to lure my dog through my legs using a treat
- To keep your dog between your legs, have a handful of treats ready. Keep giving out small bits.

- Try your best to keep your dog between your legs as long as possible
- You know you are successful when your dog gets into position when you say "center" without using a lure. Still, praise them and hand out treats now and again.

One reason why this exercise is on Week 4 of the program is that some dogs may not want to stand there. This is a sign that the bond between you and your dog is not strong enough yet. Still, if you follow Weeks 1 through 3, then your dog should be comfortable with you.

If you have problems getting your dog to get behind you, flip the script. It is a lot easier to put yourself in front of your dog than to get your dog lined up behind you. Keep moving around until your back is pointed to your dog.

Pro tip: In addition to keeping the treat flowing, give your dog a lot of praise and neck scratches to remind them that this is a safe and pleasant place to be. Sometimes, your dog will just come to you this way because they want to feel safe.

Leash Running (Advanced)

The final level of your dog leash training is to go for a run with it. If you are not used to running, consider doing it. It is also very healthy for you and provides a momentary detraction from the monotonous buzz of modern life. Going for a run clears your head and lets you think clearly as well, on top of the obvious health benefits.

But before you go running with your dog, remember that **your furry friend is very susceptible to heat.** Your dog will suffer from heatstroke before you do, so keep this in mind. Be smart and observant.

How far can a dog run? **The furthest I recommend taking your dog is 6 miles.** Not an inch farther. Smaller dogs will need to take a break far shorter than that.

When you are out running, watch out for red flags such as lagging on the leash, panting heavily with the tongue hanging out, seeking shade to lie down in, etc. Those are good signs to stop.

So, if you want to go out for a jog or run with your dog, do the following:

- Use a harness since a collar puts pressure on your dog's neck. It is a safety risk when you go fast.
- Use a bungee or coil leash to keep it away from anyone's feet or paws, making the run much safer and smoother for you and your dog
- Do not wrap the leash around your hand because you might break it in an accident
- If you run at night, having a beacon on your dog ensures that it is visible to night commuters
- Prepare some water for your dog. I use a collapsible water bowl because it is easy to carry around
- Having a short leash also keeps your dog relatively close to you in a crowded location

- Just like walking your dog on the sidewalk, put yourself on their left (or on the side closer to the street) so you can stop your dog from veering off into the street (and potential traffic!)
- If your dog loves to pull, I recommend attaching the leash to the front of their harness (search "no pull harness" on Amazon). When your dog pulls, it will be directed back to you. As a result, you stop them from pulling with no effort at all.

Remember that going for a run with your dog can be tricky. So, if this is too difficult for you, you can just settle for walking your dog instead. Even seasoned runners struggle with managing the leash, pace, and direction. You really need to keep an eye out for these things, which can be mentally taxing.

That said, if you can overcome this problem, going for frequent runs with your dog will be a very rewarding experience.

Key Takeaway

This is the final week! Training goes far beyond this, depending on how fast your dog learns but keep at it. Let's do a quick recap:

- Ask your dog to sit before you give them their meals so they do not cling onto you when you whip out the bowl
    - Only put the food down if they sit

    - Otherwise, put it away and try again 60 seconds later
- Teach your dog that they should not go into certain rooms
    - Position your dog around the doorway where you do not want your dog to enter
    - Use the “stay” command and walk away
    - Come back and reward your dog. Increase the duration next time
- The guard/center position is helpful when you need to navigate through a crowd and it also teaches your dog that they can seek safety under you
    - Stand with your back to your dog
    - Lure your dog to come and stay between your legs, pin a command
    - Try to get your dog to stay there as long as possible by giving treats
- If you want to go running with your dog, make sure to get a harness to prevent accidents
    - Position yourself closer to the street to protect your dog
    - Use short bungee or coil leash for safety
    - Have some water ready
    - Watch for signs of overheating

And that is the 4-week course complete! In the next chapter, I will tell you how you can tackle undesirable behaviors through positive redirection.

Chapter 8: Curbing Negative Behaviors

"It's easier to steer than stop a dog."

– Chad Mackin

Dogs can get a bit rowdy sometimes, and it is your job to keep them in check. Otherwise, unruly behaviors can wreak havoc in your home. Such behaviors can be dangerous for your dog and those around them.

Keep in mind that some negative behaviors will be challenging to change, such as continuous barking or marking through urination in your home. These are difficult to curb because your dog does it purely by instinct. That said, I will give you some tips to help you manage such behaviors.

At the end of the day, all the bad behaviors your dog display are not by malice. They do not really see and understand the world the same way we do. So, cut them some slacks and be patient.

It can be gratifying to punish your dog but control your frustration. Through consistency and repetition, you might be able to direct your dog in a more positive direction.

Chewing Shoes

Dogs, especially puppies, will chew your shoes, furniture, and other items that they should not have in their mouths. **It could be a sign that they have excess energy and they are trying to vent by chewing your things.** So, here is how you manage this behavior:

- Set your dog up for success by tidying up. Put your shoes and other items in places that your dog cannot get to.
- If you catch your dog red-handed, do not turn it into a game of chase since this is in a way rewarding their behavior.
- Instead, tell your dog "Drop it"
- Channel that energy elsewhere and give your dog something better, like a chew toy
- Since you can't really put away furniture, if your dog goes for those instead of the chew toys, rub wintergreen oil on them. It has a refreshing odor that dogs do not like. Don't worry. It is not dangerous to your dog in any way.

Some dogs also chew on things because they are anxious. Puppies do it for fun and will eventually grow out of it when they get older. In any case, chew toys will provide a healthier outlet for their pent-up energy. Stick to using the chew toys. If you give your old shoes to them because you just got a fresh pair, you are just teaching your dog to chew on shoes.

But what if your dog eats and swallows things like dirt, sand, clay, paper, and other non-food items? This behavior is called pica, and the only way to control it is by limiting their access to those things.

Digging

As mentioned before, dogs have many reasons to carve out a hole in the ground. Maybe they want a cool hole to rest in on a hot summer afternoon. Maybe it is just their den-making instinct. Perhaps they want to hunt a gopher, escape the yard, or bury something. Sometimes, they do it just to get a kick out of it.

Unfortunately, you cannot stop this behavior completely. Instead, what you can do is control this behavior. Consider the following:

- Designate an area that your dog can dig. Add a bit of water to soften the ground, making it much more appealing to your dog.
- To stop your dog from getting muddied, consider filling that digging spot with wood shavings or rubber mulch
- The digging area should have shade with sand or green grass, which are good for digging
- Consider investing in an elevated dog bed. It keeps your dog cooler than those on the ground. That way, your dog does not need to dig a hole.

As you can see, there is little else you can do to stop this behavior. Digging is just what dogs do. **Scolding them**

after the fact is no use. Instead, focus on ways you can prevent this behavior by allowing them to have fun in certain areas.

Pro tip: Try to understand why your dog digs in the first place. That way, you can come up with effective ways to address this behavior.

Trash Bin Digging

Does your dog love to stick its snout into trash cans? Have you come home one day to find all the trash over the house? There are many solutions, such as:

- Simply getting a better trash can. Get a pet-proof trash can that comes with locking lids. Problem solved.
- You can also give your dog a negative impression of the trash can. Get an empty can and put a few coins in.
- When your dog is neck-deep in the trash can, sneak up on your dog and shake the coin can. The sound should startle your dog and cause them to yank its head out.
- They will look at you, so hide the can and pretend as if you are just as startled as they are. Play dumb. The idea is to make your dog think that going into the trash can caused the noise.
- Redirect your dog's attention by asking them to sit and reward them with a treat or petting.

If you choose the scare tactic, remember that the result depends on how your dog responds to sudden noises. Some dogs, such as those trained to be in a firefight, may not even flinch at the abrupt sound.

Dogs are more clever than you think. I have worked with dog owners who said that their dogs could figure out how to open a trash can lid. This is why getting a trash can with a locking lid can stop this behavior in its track.

Hyper

Sometimes, your dog gets excited. Okay, maybe a little too excited. When your dog goes hyper, anything attention you give your dog, pleasant or not, will add fuel to the fire. In fact, anything you do adds fuel to the fire. So, when your dog is hyper, try the following to calm them down:

- Drop whatever it is you are doing, especially if you are playing with your dog.
- Turn your back to the dog and give them the cold shoulder treatment – ignore them.
- Your dog will be taken aback by the sudden change of tone. They will eventually calm down and come look at you.
- When your dog has calmed down, you can continue playing with your dog. Give them a treat.

Some dogs will be more hyper than others. Unfortunately, there is nothing you can do to change their personality. The solution is to teach them to give you some calmness when you ask for it. If your dog learns how to focus, as highlighted in Week 2, then you can try to get your dog to give you calm eye contact.

Barking

Barking in itself may not be bad behavior. After all, your dog may see someone at the front door and wants you to know about it. However, if it has no apparent cause and happens frequently, then it can get annoying pretty quickly. So, what can you do to control this behavior?

- Your dog may want to go outside. Maybe they need to go do their business. If so, take them outside.
- If your dog sees something they are not familiar with, it will let out an alert bark. Go look and assure your dog by saying, "It's okay. Settle down" in a calm voice.
- If your dog barks because they want your attention, do not give them any. You do not want your dog to have a habit of barking whenever they want your attention.
- If your dog barks to scare something or someone away, engage your dog when they turn to you by petting them.
- Asking your dog to lie down should also stop them from barking

Keep in mind that the ideas above only work when you are at home. There is little you can do to stop your dog from barking when you are absent other than to control the environment. That means closing the curtains so your dogs cannot see out the yard.

If you have more than one dog, then you have my condolence. When one starts barking, the others will follow suit. One way you can manage this is by finding out which dog starts barking first. Focus on training that dog using the methods above.

Some dog breeds also bark more than others. Those include fox terrier, Siberian husky, German shepherd, Yorkshire terrier, beagle, dachshund, miniature schnauzer, West Highland white terrier, and the infamous Chihuahua. **This is another reason why you need to be picky when choosing a dog breed.**

Nipping, Biting (Puppy)

Puppies usually have this urge to just bite things when their baby teeth start to grow. At that point, they will nip or bite your finger or other parts of your body eventually. What you can do is gently let them know that you do not appreciate it by:

- First, determine how hard is too hard for you to handle. Puppies have full control over how hard they can bite you.
- If it is too hard, make some noise by saying "Ow!", clutch the bitten area, and turn away.
- After 10 seconds of the cold shoulder treatment, you can interact with the pup again. Rinse and repeat.

This simple technique teaches your puppy some etiquette when playing and they will eventually learn where you draw the line. This also works on older dogs.

The funny thing about this technique is that dogs also do it among themselves. When they play with each other, and one got a little too excited and bites too hard, the other will yelp and retreat and stop the interaction. The guilty dog eventually learns that if they bite too hard, they will lose their play partner, so they stop doing that.

Marking (Peeing)

This is one of the most difficult behaviors to stop because territorial urine marking is done purely by instinct. Just like digging, **punishing your dog will not help and will only cause your dog to fear you.** Here are some ways you can control this behavior:

- Use a cleaner designed to remove urine odor to clean the affected areas as soon as possible. Your dogs will continue to urinate in those spots to re-mark them.
- Block off areas that your dog urinated on. Alternatively, try to feed and play in the areas where they do it. Dogs will not urinate where they eat, after all.
- Keep an eye on your dog. If they are about to urinate, stop them with a loud sound and take them outside to their usual spot.

- Put away other people's belongings and new items.

The last point deserves a bit of explanation. Your dog might start to mark all over the house if they see someone or something new. You might see this behavior when you have guests over. Even a new pet or regular visitor can trigger territorial urination.

Another way to minimize this behavior is by allowing your dog to get to know the other person or pet. Your dog may just feel insecure and want the other person or animal to know that it is their territory. If they understand that the new person or pet is no threat, they may no longer wish to mark their territory.

I also want to mention that spaying or neutering can also lower such incidence, but your mileage may vary. Also, if your dog has been doing this for a while, then it is going to be even more difficult to control. If you have more than one male dog, then you might run into this problem frequently as well.

Key Takeaway

- Chewing shoes: Give your dog a chew toy and put away your shoes or whatever your dog can get their paws on. For furniture legs, use wintergreen oil
- Digging: Give your dog a place for that
- Digging in the trash bin: Get a pet-proof bin
- Hyper: Do not give your dog any attention
- Barking: Ask your dog to lie down or investigate and respond accordingly

- Nipping: Make some noise, stop the activity, and do not give the pup any attention for 10 seconds
- Marking: Interrupt them with a loud noise and take them to the usual spot. Clean up the mess and try to limit access to affected areas

Conclusion

You have reached the end of this book, equipped with new knowledge and understanding of your furry friend than when you turned the first page. After these 4 weeks, your dog should be a very good boy that is well-behaved in your home. The question now is, "Now what?"

Well, now you can go out there and give your dog the best life. Give them all your love and your best care because dogs, being the loyal and lovable companions that they are, deserve nothing less.

If you do not have a dog already, why not adopt one? There are many unfortunate souls in rescue shelters that deserve a second chance at life. Though they may be a bit behind in terms of socializing and training, this 4-week program will bring them up to speed.

Whatever you do, make sure to carefully consider whether you can take care of a dog and do extensive research on which breed will be the most compatible with you. Gather all the information on dog breeds, among other things, to ensure that you get the right dog for you. Getting a dog is a huge commitment, after all. The last thing you want to think about is that you should have gotten a different breed.

Life with a dog is not always rosy. There are times when

they are annoying and tough to handle. I would know since I work with them all the time. That said, dogs do not mean any harm. Truly. There is always a reason behind every bizarre dog behavior, even if it makes no sense to humans.

Just like us, dogs have good and bad days, and their behaviors reflect that. The best thing you can do is to continue to care for them. Keep in mind that you must not use physical punishment for any reason. It does not work and only serves to ruin the relationship between you and your dog.

If there is one lesson to take away from this book about caring for your dog, it is this: treat your dogs as if they are your children. Would you hit your son if they soil the carpet?

Instead, stick to positive reinforcement. Instead of punishing your dog for what they do wrong, reward your dog for what they do right. Of course, when your dog does something wrong, there is no reward for them. This is the only acceptable punishment.

Positive reinforcement is powerful because it makes the learning process fun and rewarding both for you and your dog. It also strengthens the bond between you and your dog as well.

There are nuances to positive reinforcement that you need to remember. For one, it is a double-edged sword. You need to view the situation from your dog's point of view to avoid rewarding undesirable behavior. Something as small as your yelling to stop or your attention can be a reward in certain situations. Understand what the reward for that negative behavior could be and do not give your dog the satisfaction.

Another thing to keep in mind is that positive reinforcement is an ongoing process. You need to keep rewarding your dog when they do as they are told with treats, pets, toys, or just your attention.

At first, you will burn through a lot of treats, but you can wean them off once your dog can perform the action reliably. Your dog will still continue to follow your command because they believe that it will get treats eventually.

Another thing I want to remind you is that you want to keep training sessions short. I recommend sticking to 5-minute sessions for the best result. How many sessions per day is entirely up to you, but keep in mind that there is only so much a dog can learn in a day.

Your first week with your dog is all about helping them settle in. The first day should be kept calm and low-key, and let your dog explore their new home. From there, you need to start working on the basics, such as potty training, crate training, and feeding. These take the longest, so you want to start early.

In the second week, other than making sure your dog gets plenty of socialization, it is all about basic commands such as sit down, walking with a leash, and asking for their attention.

For the third week, you can start working on more complex commands like stay, come, drop it, leave it, and have a trial run (or walk) outside with your dog on a leash.

In the final week, you can instill some discipline and manners in your dog using the commands from previous weeks. For instance, teaching your dog to sit before they have their meals, respecting off-limit areas, going on a run on a leash, and taking the guard/center position.

When it comes to curbing negative behaviors, the idea is pretty simple. You address the root cause or provide a healthier/tolerable alternative behavior for your dog. Some behaviors are done purely based on instinct and will be difficult to control, if not impossible.

Make absolutely sure that you maintain consistency when training your dog. You want to use the same cues every time and give the reward at the same moment every time. Through repetition and consistency, your dog will learn eventually. It will take time, so be patient.

Of course, we would be here all day if we go over every single trick a dog could learn. But you should have an idea of how to teach your dog different behaviors using positive reinforcement, so you can definitely get your dog to perform new tricks like shaking your hand.

I do not include those because this is only meant to be a 4-week program to get the fundamentals out of the way. That said, dogs are incredibly smart creatures, and they can learn to do all sorts of things except doing taxes.

With all that said, I wish you and your canine companion the very best. From one dog owner to another, the last tip I will give you from one dog owner to another is this: have fun!

BOOK 2

Complete Mental Exercises for Dogs Handbook

20+ Exercises to Stimulate Your Dog's Mind and Boost Mental Health!

Brianna Ramirez

Book 2 Description

Are you looking for **endless fun** for your dear canine companion? A happy dog is a mentally and physically spent dog. Games are important to keep your dog fit and content. **Walks aren't enough**. Just like humans, they also need something more.

There are many indoor and outdoor activities to entertain your canine companion, not to mention that they will also be fit and well-behaved. And if your dog has a myriad of activities to keep busy, they will stay away from undesirable behaviors**. It is a win-win**. If you are looking for fun games to play and bond with your dog, look no further!

Fortunately, **dogs do not need much to have their needs met**. You do not need special training or any fancy equipment. You can use things laying around the house to make games that challenge your dog and get them to think creatively.

Certified and expert dog trainer, Brianna Ramirez, provides you with **a comprehensive, easy-to-follow, step-by-step guide for a variety of games suitable for dogs of all shapes and sizes**. It does not matter what your dog's breed or temperament is, there is a game for them.

All of these games also double as training for your dog to instill discipline through tried-and-true positive reinforcement and clicker training. Your dog would learn and have fun at the same time which is the best approach to teaching!

In **Complete Mental Exercises for Dogs Handbook**, you will find:

- Why dogs need both physical and mental exercise
- What your dog needs to be happy
- The right way to teach your dog
- How to adjust to your dog's playstyle based on their archetype
- Tips to make the most out of each exercise
- Solutions for problematic behavior during playing
- Over 20 exercises
- ... And so much more!

So, what are you waiting for? Join in with your canine companion! Have fun!

Imagine all the fun you can have with your dog and the amazement when you show your friends and family cool tricks your dog can perform. Start today and build a foundation for your dog's fitness and mental finesse!

Get fit and bond with your dog with **Complete Mental Exercises for Dogs Handbook.**

Introduction

"The bond with a true dog is as lasting as the ties of this earth will ever be." - *Orhan Pamuk*

Does your dog chew on your shoes? Do they dig up the entire backyard as if they are looking for oil? Do these behaviors make you think that your dog has a bone to pick with you?

I will tell you right now that your dog does not hate you. They have nothing against you. What they do have a lot of is boredom.

Dogs are very intelligent and complex creatures. They are a lot like humans in the sense that they have different needs, skills, and interests. And just like humans, they are not going to be fully satisfied with just food, water, and shelter.

All of the above are crucial for survival, but survival does not equate to happiness. We need something to do. Dogs also have the same needs. And the kind of entertainment you provide your dog is very important.

Now, I know what you are thinking. All the bad behaviors I mentioned at the start cannot possibly be caused by boredom, right? Well, I will give you another human example.

You can go on Google and search "self-inflicted pain out of boredom" and you will be greeted by numerous scientific studies on boredom itself. Long story short, participants, **human participants, would rather hurt themselves via electric shock rather than endure another second of boredom**.

Think about it. We would rather harm ourselves to break up the monotony. So, it is not far-fetched to argue that **your dog digs up your backyard because they are just bored**, and all the behavioral studies on canine support this idea.

In many cases, bad behaviors can be stopped or at least controlled by simply giving your dog a healthier outlet such as toys to keep them busy. And the responsibility falls to you as a dog owner to provide them with sufficient entertainment.

What is interesting about dogs is that they prefer humans as their social partners over fellow pups. That is not to say that dogs do not get socialization development from fellow dogs, but they certainly will not get optimal development without human intervention.

As you can probably tell by now, your dog relies on you in more ways than one. Other than their basic needs for food, water, and shelter, they also rely on you to teach them the ways of the world and to care for their overall well-being.

Of course, if it is a world ruled by dogs, then your dog would not need your help. They can learn social etiquette from fellow dogs and that would be enough. But this is a world dominated by humans. So, in this shared world, your dog needs you to guide them, and help them understand how to behave around humans.

Looking at other species such as wolves and hyenas, you would know that dogs are meant to move around a lot. They had to go back to ancient times. They spent all day stalking, chasing, and hunting down prey.

Dogs back in the day had to keep track of a lot of things when they hunt. All of this is mentally taxing and after a successful hunt, they would just lie down and rest.

The need to move is still present in dogs today. Of course, some dogs need to stretch their limbs more than others. But taking your dog out for a walk is not going to be enough.

My name is Brianna Ramirez, a certified dog training expert. I have been around dogs for as long as I could remember. I must confess that I did not fully understand a dog's needs until I decided to follow this career path. We still know so little about dogs that one can be forgiven for assuming that a dog is satisfied with just a short walk.

I have worked with all sorts of dogs from timid to energetic, from the smallest and angriest chihuahua to the biggest yet gentlest Great Dane. I am not saying that my early days were perfect nor can I fully understand dogs even now, but I currently know much more about them compared to the time I applied to be a dog trainer.

Though working with these lovable creatures sounds like a dream, there have been highs and lows in my career. But what is important is that I learned a great deal on the job, and I am here to share with you everything I've learned.

I believe that raising a dog is similar to raising kids in the sense that you will not be short of advice. Unfortunately, not all of them are good advice. **One of the biggest mistakes dog owners make is assuming that a dog is sufficiently entertained from a 30-minute walk.** So, I wrote this book not only to dispel this misinformation but to educate and raise awareness about dog care.

Just like children, you would want the best for your dogs as well. Take good care of your dog and the reward is something that even money cannot buy. There is no one I know whose life is made worse after they got a dog.

In this book, I will give you all the fun ideas to keep boredom at bay for your dog. You will find all sorts of games that are exciting and stimulating for your dog.

Not only that, but these activities also help you understand your canine companion even more. You see, these games also require your involvement. **By playing with your dog, not only does the bond between you grow stronger, but you will also be able to interpret your dog's reaction with greater accuracy.**

Moreover, these activities are not just idle fun and games.

They are designed to challenge your dog's intelligence, endurance, and discipline as well. For you, the benefit is that you will develop a greater understanding of your pup.

At the end of the day, these exercises should teach your dog how to be an attentive and disciplined companion who is eager to follow your lead. Will these make your dog "smarter"? Probably not. But they will broaden your dog's horizons and set them up to be an all-around good dog with an interesting personality and keen discipline, which makes a dog "smart".

Chapter 1: The Importance of Play

"A dog will teach you unconditional love. If you can have that in your life, things won't be too bad." – Robert Wagner

A lot of dog owners and trainers preach that a good dog is a tired dog. To be precise, if you take them out for walks and tire them out, they would no longer have the energy to pursue destructive habits. That is only partially true.

Yes, if your dog has too much energy they need to burn, they would go after your shoe or furniture or practice archaeology in the backyard. But just because you tire them out by taking them out on long walks does not mean they will stop.

Let's flip the script so you can understand what is really going on. What does a dog need? Food, water, and shelter are a must. Exercising is also important. But is that all? What if that is all you have in your life? Would you be happy?

Hardly, of course. Sure, your physical needs are met, but what do you do with all the time you have? Me, I would be bored out of my mind. I certainly would not be happy or content. Yes, that bit of exercise is stimulating but going for a run now and again is not what anyone would consider fun.

The same applies to your pup. **There is always a reason behind a dog's behavior and there are no bad dogs, just misunderstood ones.** Dogs need to be exhausted mentally as well if you want to curb bad behavior.

Dogs think a lot more like humans than we realize. If they are bored and have nothing to do, they will eventually turn to undesirable behavior. To make matters worse, guess what? If your dog is physically fit, then they even have more energy to do bad things. Instead of chewing through one shoe, they can go through 20 by the time you said "Drop it!"

Okay, maybe not 20 shoes, but you get the idea. I am not saying that walks are ineffective. But those alone are inadequate. Yes, taking your dog out provides a change in scenery and lets them interact with other humans and animals. But how much time can you realistically spend a day on walks?

What would your dog do between each walk? Surely, they would need something fun to do. And if you do not provide any, they will find one themselves, and that is usually something you do not approve of.

So, as a dog owner, you also need to provide sufficient mental stimuli to keep your dog busy. The good news is that dogs perceive fun differently from humans.

Some of us read literature, watch movies, play computer games, and browse the internet to pass the time. Dogs don't need any of that, so you do not need to invest in a gaming console for them. They can get by with simple toys and exercises.

Safety Advice

Although we will go over loads of activities in this book, what you can do together with your dog for fun is pretty much limitless. But before you do anything, it is important to stay safe. Accidents do happen and a prudent dog owner would do everything to minimize that risk.

Age and Fitness

Dogs will get tired at some point although where that point is depends on the dog's age and overall fitness. All of them can play games and have fun but do not push them too far. This is important for old dogs and very young pups.

Dogs that are still in the growing and developing stage, which is between 1 to 2 years of age should not strain themselves too much. They should not be jumping, either. They do not know that, so the responsibility falls to you to recognize how much play is enough.

The same can be said for older dogs. You wouldn't expect an 80-year-old man to be able to play basketball. For dogs, anywhere above 10 years old is considered old, but that really depends on the breed. Regardless, older dogs should not be overexcited to the point they hurt themselves, either.

Things such as jumping, standing and walking on their hind legs, and turning awkwardly can lead to long-term strain or injury. My best advice here is to use common sense to judge what is suitable for your dog.

Know Your Dog

This should be quite easy considering that you are the closest to your dog. You would know what your dog loves and hates. You should have a good idea of your dog's tendencies and temperament. All of these will be important when coming up with games for your dog.

For instance, if your dog is competitive and likes to one-up everybody, you need to be careful in introducing competitive games like tug of war. If your dog likes to guard their favorite toys, you might want to teach them how to drop their toys or swap them before introducing them to toy-based games.

Another important thing to remember is that not all dogs respond to the same game with an equal amount of enthusiasm. Just like how humans have unique preferences, dogs too may enjoy some games more than others.

So, if your dog does not seem particularly interested in a certain game, even if it seems fun to you, do not push it.

Instead, try a different game. Do not worry. I have included a wide variety of games here so I am sure at least one of them will light the spark in your pup.

Plus, your dog would learn easily and have more fun if you focus on what they are good at.

Dogs and Children

Dogs can get along with children very well. There are countless videos on YouTube to prove that. Still, children do not understand dogs and dogs do not understand humans much either. So, playtime can be unpredictable.

This is why you should always supervise playtime when children and dogs are involved. **Do not leave a young child with a dog.** If excitement runs high, children might start to get rough and your dog might respond with the same amount of enthusiasm. This can lead to injury for your dog and children.

Observe

Cross-species play usually goes awry when one side does not understand the body language of another. In this case, the responsibility falls to you to watch your dog's body language during playtime. It is a good idea to develop this habit of being observant so you can understand how they behave and make an accurate guess whether your dog is having fun or not.

More importantly, to an untrained eye, it is difficult to

see whether two dogs going at it are actually playing or a full-on brawl. That way, you can swoop in and interrupt if things get out of hand or stay back if the dogs are just having a lot of fun together.

Keep in mind that every dog is different. Some dogs may find fetch to be fun and engaging whereas others just find it outright boring. This is why I included a wide variety of games to cater to pretty much every dog. Get to know your pup and figure out what clicks.

What Dogs Think About Play

Humans and dogs love to play, so we at least have that in common. If you have spent any time around dogs at all, you would realize that a lot of things come naturally like a game of chase. Dogs just love to play since, well, they do not have a 9 to 5 job as we do.

Play comes to dogs naturally and puppies start to explore their strange new world when they are three weeks of age. They use their mouths and paws to investigate every little thing, if not getting into a bit of rough and tumble with their littermates. By the time they are a month old, all the time they spend other than sleeping and eating will be used for playing and exploration.

At first, small puppies will spend their time playing with their mother who will teach them some play etiquette. For instance, the mother will paw away a puppy that bites too hard. These natural behaviors build the foundation of dog behaviors later on.

As they grow, puppies will spend time playing with their siblings. Just by watching them, you will see some familiar games such as chase and rollover with other puppies, or they will play alone with some toys such as a ball.

These behaviors are important because the games I described above are based on dogs' natural behaviors. **These exercises serve as a practice for life as an adult dog when they find themselves in the wild.** A dog has to hunt for their own food and these games prepare them for that.

Such behaviors are not uncommon in other mammal species. Young mammals also share the same enthusiasm for play but they tend to lose it as they mature.

However, both humans and dogs understand that they can still play just for the pleasure of the moment. 99% of dogs I have worked with can be encouraged into some form of play and dogs can read the mood of their partner as well. They can tell if their play partner has the same intent to play or not.

For instance, a common sign of playful invitation is the bow and maybe a bit of wiggle or tail swings. Or, your dog could drop down and show you their stomach and a slack jaw to tell you that they will just playfully nip you.

You do learn a lot about your dog's behavior just by watching them play. It is even better if they have another dog as a playmate so you can see how they interact.

This is why taking your dog to a care center might be a good idea so you can observe your dog's behavior. Alternatively, if you own one dog, you can set up a playdate with another dog owner, just make sure that the first couple of sessions are with dogs of a similar size.

Training and Playing

Back when we did not really understand dogs, we used to think that training and playing with your dog are two different things. To humans, it sort of makes sense.

We train so we can do the hard work and playing can be considered to be some sort of reward that we enjoy after a long day of work. But we are just applying human concepts to dogs, and that usually does not work well. **We need to see things from their perspective.**

To dogs, there are no reasons why they cannot learn and have fun at the same time. Games can strengthen your bond and teach your dog to be more attentive, which makes life with a pup all the more enjoyable.

The question then becomes whether your dog can tell the difference. Simply put, no, not really. Studies suggest that dogs' distanced awareness does not extend far. Distanced awareness is the degree that the subject can see themselves from a third person's perspective. Dogs are, understandably, not very good at such a complex thought.

So, when you are hunting with your dog, they won't be wondering if they are playing or learning. They know for a fact that they are interacting with you and that they are having a good time. And they just want to find the next treat.

Dogs live in the moment and do not think too hard about their situation. So long as it leads to positive outcomes, your dog would be happy. In this case, your dog will be focused on finding the treat which requires a bit of thinking on their part. As the game gets tougher, they may turn their attention to you for some hints.

For this particular game, you are hitting two birds with one stone. Not only do you train your dog to think but also teach your dog to focus on you. That is on top of the fact that you two are doing an enjoyable activity, so it is a win-win situation.

Where Does the Training Come into It?

Of course, the goal of these exercises is to challenge your dog mentally. So, your dog must gain something other than entertainment from them. The training mainly applies every time you start to play with your dog. **At that precise moment, they are learning to read your signals.**

If you play with your dog with a specific goal in mind, you can use it to improve your dog's concentration. Again, dogs live in the moment and they can lose focus quickly.

It also helps strengthen the bond between you and your dog as well.

In addition, you also send clear signals to your dog and they can understand you better and better. They understand what you want them to do and that it will have a positive outcome. They get treats for following your command. This is positive reinforcement and it works.

Do Dogs Learn Differently?

Dogs mostly learn the same way but the thing that sets them apart is the fact that they all have different personalities. Some are just more wired to do better in certain activities than others. **For this reason, you should engage your dogs with exercises that are suitable for their strengths.**

For instance, if your dog goes from 0 to 100 whenever you show them their favorite squeaky toy and you want them to be a little less hyper during playtime, there is a game for that. I will show you in a later chapter, but this game can help your pet focus without getting too overexcited.

Even with this game, your dog will still think that they are playing and they will be playing toward the goal that you want.

Key Takeaway

- Playing is essential in keeping your dog away from undesirable behavior that stems from boredom
- To a dog, training and playing are the same things if they have fun
- Even when playing, your dog at least learns to observe your behavior
- Every dog is different in how they respond to a particular game. Observe and alter your strategy accordingly
- Consider your dog's age and fitness to determine appropriate games

In the next chapter, we will discuss how your dog's breed can influence their behavior and what you should expect.

Chapter 2: Understanding Your Pup

"It's not only about dog training. It's about people training too."

– Leila Grandemange

A few centuries ago, everybody would assume that all dogs had a job such as herding sheep or hunting rats. Nowadays, every dog has a solid heritage that we can track and this gives us an idea of how they behave.

Does the breed influence how a dog plays? Science cannot give us a clear answer just yet, but what I observe is that it does to some extent. Your dog's behavior can be estimated based on their breed origins, whether it is a purebred or a mixed breed. So, let's talk about that.

Dog Categorization

Dogs are categorized into different breeds based on what functions the breeds used to serve. This is a standard set by most national kennel clubs. They vary slightly between communities in terms of naming and how dogs are categorized.

For instance, the American Kennel Club has a category called the Herding Group. In the United Kingdom, that would be the Pastoral category. Regardless, these classifications make it convenient to guess what tendencies your dog may have.

The AKC's categories are Herding, Hound, Non-Sporting, Sporting, Terrier, Toy, and Working. The UK used different names: Gundog, Hound, Pastoral, Terrier, Toy, and Utility.

Yes, I know what you are probably thinking. Stereotyping is wrong and I've always preached that all dogs are different even if they are of the same breed. But hear me out.

Yes, I do agree that categorizing dogs like this can be misleading. We do not fully understand dogs yet and so these classifications are going to be inaccurate. Keeping this in mind, I highly advise you to take this with a grain of salt. My advice is to just use this as a general guide to shape your expectations.

The classification is not going to tell you everything you need to know about your dog. What it can do is give you some idea of what you can expect from your dog in terms of play style and personality. Understanding your dog's breed can at least help you anticipate problems in training and teaching.

Categories

With that in mind, here is a short list of main dog groups based on different kennel clubs. Again, how they name and categorize dogs vary slightly but this is the general definition:

- Herding/pastoral: Dogs bred to herd and guard livestock. Includes Border Collie, Corgis, etc. So, you can expect the characteristics to vary wildly. Some breeds have stronger herding instincts than others.
- Hound: These dogs are bred to hunt. Two subcategories exist for hounds. Scent hounds are used for tracking, so they have very sensitive noses even by dog standards. Sighthounds are best at chasing as they pack a lot of speed.
- Terrier: These dogs specialize in hunting small prey or vermin. They are energetic, determined, and sometimes a bit stubborn.
- Toy: These dogs are intended to be companions and not much else and many small breeds fall into this category.
- Working: These are large dogs that perform guarding or search-and-rescue work. Highly intelligent and gentle, working breeds include the Doberman Pinscher, St. Bernard, and Newfoundland.
- Sporting/Gundog: These dogs are bred for hunting purposes such as sighting, flushing a game out, or retrieving it after it has been shot. They have keen eyesight and a sensitive nose. This category covers breeds such as retrievers, pointers, and spaniels.
- Non-sporting/utility: Generally applies to dogs that do not fit any of the above categories. Some of them

do have a purpose but it is usually very specific. This is where a lot of exceptions can be found because it is impossible to generalize these breeds.

Stereotyping

If you have a purebred dog, then you will hear this very often: "This behavior is common for dogs of this breed". Other dog owners will tell you that it is just how your dog is supposed to be. Toy dogs will have a Napoleon complex, terriers will be noisy, energetic, and stubborn, and Spaniels will follow their noses.

To those who do not have a lot of experience around dogs, these statements start to sound more and more truthful the more they are repeated. But I urge you not to listen to other people.

The categories above just give you a few ideas of what you can expect from your dog. **But ultimately, your experience with your dog may vary.** It partly depends on what you do with your dog.

So, a toy dog may have a Napoleon complex but this is only reinforced by the fact that the owner just accepts it. Maybe the dog does not have a Napoleon complex but the owner unwittingly reinforces it. Neither you nor I can know for sure.

What I certainly know is that there are always exceptions so do not let the labels blind you to what your dog does. Just because the breed loves hunting games does not mean that they do not enjoy puzzles. Experiment and see what works with your dog.

Personality

Whether or not your dog conforms to their breed standard does not matter. Your dog is unique – an individual. Sure, maybe they will grow up to be your stereotypical retriever, but they still have a unique personality.

As a dog owner, only you know your dog best. I have worked with many dogs in the past, their respective owners are more familiar with them than I do. After all, you as the owner get to spend a lot more time with your dog.

So, it is very unlikely that anyone else other than you know your dog better. If you start paying more attention to your dog, you can make an educated guess as to whether your dog would accept and adapt to new ideas even before you start introducing them.

The dog's breed can give you an estimation of a dog's behavior, but every dog in that breed will behave differently. So, if you have a litter of Golden Retrievers, every single one of them is going to be different. Though Golden Retrievers are known for their people skills and trainability, some will be shy and others will be stubborn.

Every dog breeder will tell you that a dog's personality will always differ from the norm. So, how dogs approach exercises will differ.

"Smart" Dogs

Many dog trainers I know usually joke when dog owners boast about how "smart" their dog is. To that, we say "unlucky". Why is that?

Well, there is nothing wrong with a smart dog per se. But dogs that can think for themselves will be tricky to train and play with since they can think for themselves and they may prefer to do something else.

Instances of independent dogs like this can vary across breeds but I encounter some now and again regardless of the dog breed. In both training and play, they are more challenging compared to dogs that do not care and just want to follow your guidance.

Timid or Scaredy Dogs

Though some dogs are born shy or fearful, others' timid personalities can be explained by under-socialization when they were puppies. During that time, your dog may not get enough opportunities to familiarize themselves with their strange new world.

Regardless, this type of dog is usually apprehensive and prefers a quiet life. If your dog falls into this type, then play and exercise should be introduced slowly, and do not coerce them into doing anything they clearly do not want to do. A slow approach with rewards can persuade the shyest dog into doing things that are worth learning.

Confident Dogs

This type of dog is usually the easiest to train. They are confident enough to take the initiative but are willing to follow directions. They are also keen to interact with you and think that something new is something fun. If you have such a dog at home, then teaching them new tricks and games should not be too challenging.

"Obsessive" Dogs

Your dog may develop some sort of obsession with certain aspects of an activity. For instance, if you play fetch with your dog with a tennis ball, they may only want to play with that and nothing else. If that is the case, you need to stop this behavior early before the attachment gets out of hand. You can do this by keeping the activities and toys varied so that their focus is moved away from the subject of their obsession.

Dealing with a Toy-Obsessed Dog

All dogs have a favorite toy. But it becomes a problem when a dog likes a particular toy too much to the point of obsession. How can you tell the difference?

Favorites vs Obsessive

If a dog has a favorite toy, they will carry it around with them all day. They might even bring it to bed with them. Your dog will show signs of excitement when you use it in a game of fetch.

But if your dog is obsessed with a certain toy, they display signs of intense and extreme attachment to the point that they cannot relax around it or in a situation where they have access to it.

Such behaviors are common among working dogs that are traditionally used to herd or hunt and they have a combination of concentration and intelligence.

Obsession is not limited to toys, either. It can also apply to activities. Some dogs may be digging obsessively, chasing after light like a cat, etc. The object or activity of their obsession no longer brings them joy. It makes your dog anxious instead, which is pretty visible.

If your dog is obsessed with a certain toy, they may not want you to pick it up. If they have it, they might guard it jealously and not want you to interact with them. If it is an activity, your dog may growl and generally display displeasure if you interrupt them.

What to Do

If you see signs that your dog is developing an obsession, you need to deal with it quickly. **It is not something that your dog will grow out of.** If anything, this obsession can grow stronger over time.

There are many possible solutions depending on what your dog is obsessed with and how strong it is. **The general idea is to redirect your dog's attention elsewhere.**

This is the general strategy when you want to correct your dog's behavior. Instead of trying to put a stop to something, offer your dog a healthier, more desirable alternative. Here are some suggestions to help your dog overcome their obsession:

- Make sure that your dog gets enough exercise and play. Obsession tends to develop when they have too much mental energy. Long walks and energy-intensive games can quickly burn through a dog's energy pool.
- If your dog is fixated on a certain toy, wait until they no longer pay attention and remove it. Does it seem cruel? Not really. The toy does not give your dog joy and taking it away might even give them relief.
- If your dog develops an obsession with an activity, try to get them to work on an energy-intensive game first before letting them work on that activity. Even then, make sure to keep it short and for only a set amount of time.

Avoid the following mistakes:

- Do not try to take the object of their obsession away when they are around. They might try to stop you or just guard it against you. Trying to take it away can end poorly. Wait until your dog leaves it eventually and you can go in and switch it for something new and exciting.
- Do not reflect your dog's excitement when you are

trying to limit your dog's activity that they are obsessed with. Instead, pretend that you are prepared to engage in the activity but you are not enthusiastic about it.
- Do not limit your dog's choices of toys and games. Make sure there are enough alternatives so that you can redirect your dog's attention.

Key Takeaway

- Dog categorization, though does not give a complete picture of your dog's behavior, is still handy in helping you determine what behaviors to expect.
- Use the personality traits above to help you pick exercises that cater to their strengths.
- Ultimately, what activities you end up with depend on your dog's actual personality.

In the next chapter, we will go over everything else you need to know about training/playing with your dog.

Chapter 3: Other Playtime Essentials

"There is no point to practice when you are not ready to learn."

– Ivan Balabanov

In this chapter, we shift the focus from your dog to you as a dog trainer. I will tell you everything you need to know to set your dog up for success such as how to conduct yourself around dogs since much of your success relies on whether you are sending the right signals.

What You Need to Do

When you are teaching your dog a new trick or a new game and problems come up, it is convenient to blame the dog for not getting it or that they are just being slow. But before you put the blame on the dog, ensure you check what you are doing yourself.

Chances are that you might confuse your dog or send them mixed signals by how you are behaving. There are many common mistakes that humans make that arise from our body language.

Of course, do not be so hard on yourself for not understanding the dog and making these mistakes.

Everybody makes mistakes. Even dog trainers like me slip up from time to time.

Instead, focus on what you want to do here. You are trying to teach your dog new things and something goes wrong. **Focus on solving the problem instead of placing blames.** Maybe you need to adapt your approach to help your dog understand. Perhaps you just need to be clear and firm with your body language so your dog can follow. This section is intended to help you figure that out.

Body Language

Dogs cannot speak, at least not the same way humans can. They mainly use body language to communicate. That much is obvious. But what people do not know is that because dogs rely on body language, they become very good at observing it.

On the flip side, humans communicate using both words and body language. We are not as reliant on using our body language to convey an idea, so we do not have as much experience in expressing ourselves through body language. At least, not as much compared to dogs.

What tends to happen is that dogs can read our body language in more detail and this can lead them to draw the wrong conclusion. **So, pay more attention to your posture and your hands.** Check to make sure whether you are moving around or not.

When I first started training dogs, I would have someone watch me to see if I am doing something I should not do with my body. That way, I could be absolutely certain that I sent the right signals to the dogs I work with. You can apply the same technique at home, or record the training session with your phone. That way, you can revisit the clip later and see if you did something you should not.

What Did You Say?

Because dogs communicate primarily using their body language, our verbal instructions only play a small part in the training. It is actually difficult to stick to short instructions because, again, we tend to assume dogs can understand our language. Most people tend to repeat the instruction or command.

So, instead of saying "Come", people might say "Come here, Luke. Come on, boy. Here, to me", etc. To dogs, all of that is just gibberish. It is no wonder then that dogs look to you for clues expressed in your body language to figure out what you want them to do.

Voice and Body Dissonance

So, when training your dog or teaching them how to play a game, consistency is key. You will hear this a lot in this book, but I cannot stress this enough. Consistency here means that you must stick to using the same verbal and physical cues for a particular command. So, for "sit", you can say “sit” and point to the ground, but for “down”, you say “down”, present your palm and lower it, for example.

As you can see, each command has a unique verbal cue and a physical gesture. That way, you send clear signals to your dog about what you want them to do.

Why is this important? Because **you cannot decide what the signal is.** Your dog does, and unfortunately, you cannot just tell your dog what the signal is. They will look at you and they will figure out, or at least try to, what the signal is. If you present very few but clear signals, it makes it a lot easier for your dog.

So, how can you confuse your dog? Let’s go back to that “sit” command. Suppose that you point down and say “sit”, but unconsciously nod your head as you say “sit”, your dog might assume that the head nod is the signal and not your hand.

When you teach your dog to lie down by saying “down” and you nod your head again, your dog will be confused. You nodded your head, which they think is the gesture for “sit”, but you said “down”, which is what you want your dog to do.

Guess what? Your body language takes precedence because that is the language your dog is most familiar with. So instead of lying down, your dog just sits down and expects some sort of reward.

Therefore, pay very close attention when you are working with your dog.

Consistency also applies to the timing of the reward as well. Make sure you give your dog the reward at the exact same moment.

Using Toys

Some of the games and exercises in this book will require the use of toys. Ideally, you would use the ones that your dog is already interested in. Whether your dog has a large collection of toys or a few plastic bottles, you will need props for most exercises. Knowing your dog's favorite toys can also give you an idea of what kind of activity they like as well.

Safe Toys

First and most importantly, make sure that your dog's toys are safe for them. It is more than just grabbing whatever toys that have a "Safe for pets" label on them, though. The labels can lie and some are not well made or strong enough, especially chew toys.

One toy I recommend avoiding is rope toys. Some are made with inappropriate material or with little quality check that they break apart. Even worse still, your dog may ingest the little bits of rope and cause intestinal blockage.

Instead, just get one of those squeaky chew toys or if your dog really loves rope toys, make absolutely sure that it is a high-quality toy. From observing how your dog plays, you should have a good idea of how much they love to chew and how strong their jaws are. So, you can tell which toy is sturdy enough.

Different Kinds of Toys

They say that variety is the spice of life and you want to make your dog's life exciting, right? So, get a few different toy types for your dog. Think about what your dog likes most.

For instance, fetch games will be easier to teach your dog if you have a toy that your dog likes to pick up. Some dogs may like playing with a toy that squeaks. You can use this to your advantage by teaching your dog self-control by only giving them such toys to play with when they do what you tell them to do.

A ball is a must-have. Every dog loves it. It can be a small tennis ball or a basketball. Again, make sure that it is safe for your dog. A large dog like a Great Dane may accidentally swallow a tennis ball while playing with it, so maybe a soccer ball is more appropriate for them. If you use a basketball or a soccer ball, make sure it is inflated to avoid puncture while playing.

You can use a ball as momentary entertainment between training sessions where your dog has exerted themselves mentally. They can have a bit of fun with the ball in a game of catch or chase to clear their head and then have another go at training after.

If you have to run some errands and are worried that your dog might misbehave in your absence, you need to find a way to keep them busy. One of the most effective ways to do this would be a Kong-type toy. It has a tough rubber exterior with a hollowed inside that you can fill with food.

Food is a great motivator for dogs in training, so your dog will be busy figuring out how to get the food out of the toy while you go do something else.

If your dog has a strong chomper, maybe a chew toy might not be the best option for them. I have seen dogs destroying toys that I thought were indestructible.

At the end of the day, what toy you give your dog depends on many factors. It is up to you to observe your dog's behavior and use common sense to figure out what toys would be appropriate for them.

Toys as Rewards

Some dogs are not as motivated when presented with food. Maybe they have just been fed and treats no longer look enticing. Maybe they just do not care too much about food. Regardless, toys can be an effective alternative.

Make sure that your dog knows that you have the toys, even if it has nothing to do with the exercise or game. You can still use them to reward your dog. You can leave it in sight and look at it when you ask your dog to do something. Then, when they do what you asked, you can go grab the toy and hand it to them.

What about Wooden Sticks?

We have seen this way too often, especially in cartoons. It sort of makes sense at a glance, but veterinarians will tell you that letting your dog play with a wooden stick is one of the worst things you can do.

If your dog is a stick lover, give them a rubber stick to play with instead of grabbing a fallen branch. Wooden sticks can break and splinters are nasty. Even worse still, your dog may ingest the bits of wood or even the splinters which is painful for your dog and expensive for you to extract.

So, err on the side of caution and get a rubber stick.

Watch Your Tone

Training is more effective if you take the time to prepare. If you have seen a dog trainer in action, you will realize that you need to do a fair bit of work behind the scenes to deliver good lessons and results. In fact, this applies to pretty much every teaching job, dogs or humans. It is not as simple as showing up and teaching immediately without any preparation.

For dog training, you want to pay close attention to your spoken language and body language, especially the latter.

You might find that even simple exercises in this book will contain excruciating details. The idea is to provide you with enough details so that you can go through each exercise carefully.

Dogs struggle mainly because the exercise or trick is not taught consistently or carefully enough. To make the most of your time, consider how you are going to approach the activity before you begin. I ask myself these questions and you should too:

- **What word(s) will I use?** People tend to explain their instructions instead of giving a short verbal direction, although the latter is more effective in teaching dogs. So, if you are teaching your dog to "sit", say "sit" once or twice and nothing else. It makes everything clear to your dog and gives you the opportunity to watch yourself so that you are not confusing them with your body language.
- **What tone should I use?** There are only two that you can use: happy and firm. Or, in dog's language, high and low energy. You should sound happy to show your dog that you like interacting with them, but not too excited to avoid overstimulating them. This enthusiastic tone can be used for active exercises and games. On the flip side, a firm tone indicates to your dog that you want them to concentrate. It is low and relatively quiet to reflect your intention. Your dog might get overexcited during a game, but I urge you not to raise your voice. To your dog, it sounds as if you are just barking alongside them.

- **What pose should I assume?** If your intention is to get your dog to come to you, try learning backward slightly instead of looming over them. They might find it intimidating.

Rules of Engagement

Your dog cannot tell the difference between training and playing if they are having fun. We would not learn anything if the lesson is boring and the same principle applies to dogs. So, make your time with your dog productive and enjoyable by following these rules.

- **Do not start a training or playing session if your dog is already tired or in a bad mood.** On the flip side, if your dog is hyper, you want to burn off the extra bit of energy. Otherwise, they would be too scatterbrained to do anything that requires an ounce of focus. That's why you should consider doing 10 minutes of exercise or so after a daily walk to take the edge off.
- **Only teach your dog when you are in the right frame of mind.** If you are feeling peeved or impatient, your dog will pick it up during training and the session would not be productive, if at all successful.
- **Try different exercises in every session.** Even if you limit your session to 5 minutes once a day every day, squeeze in one exercise that your dog is familiar with and one that is new to them. If you

can commit 10 minutes a day, then have 2 exercises that your dog knows and 1 new exercise.

- If you are teaching your dog a complex exercise, you need to **divide it into stages and teach it separately** before you ask your dog to do everything together. Otherwise, you end up confusing your dog.
- **Alternate between thinking exercises and active games.** Many dog trainers and owners I work with say that they get better results if they change the pace when they teach.
- **If your dog does not understand what you want them to do, do not force the agenda.** If you have tried something 3 times and your dog still does not do what you want them to, your dog might start to get frustrated. In such a case, ask your dog to do something they are fluent in such as "sit". Any trick or command will do. What you want to accomplish here is to take the pressure off and stop your dog from becoming too anxious. You can try again the next day.
- **The rewards must be worthwhile for your dog.** You can keep the treats small but make sure that they are your dog's favorite treat. You are going to burn through a fair bit of treats, so cut back on their meals if necessary so they do not gain weight.
- **Surprise your dog with a bonus once or twice every week.** Dog trainers use this trick all

the time. Normally, when your dog does what you ask, they get a treat. But sometimes, you can give them a lot more like 5 treats at once. Your dog would be over the moon and the possibility of a treat jackpot will get your dog to focus even harder on pleasing you.

- On the flip side, **space out the treats for the exercises that your dog is already good at.** Yes, keep giving them treats, but not every time, and definitely not their favorite treat. You want to keep the good stuff for new tricks.
- **Dog training never ends.** There will come a point where you have taught your dog everything you want them to do but that does not mean you can stop training your dog. Instead, you can use those sessions to reinforce their habits, revisit exercises, and strengthen your bond.

Key Takeaway

- Your body and verbal language are key in dog training. Make absolutely sure that you stick to using the same cues and do not make any unnecessary sounds or actions so as not to confuse your dog.
- Pick the right toys for your dog. Consider the size, durability, and quality appropriate for them. Make sure to have a variety of them to keep your dog busy with different activities.
- Remember the rules of engagements:

- Only train when you and your dog are in the right frame of mind
- Try different exercises every session
- For complex exercises, split them up, teach each component individually, and then combine them
- Make sure the reward is worthwhile for your dog
- Keep the good treats for new and difficult exercises
- Switch up between action and thinking games
- Surprise your dog with a treat jackpot by giving more than usual once in a while
- Even when you have nothing new to teach your dog, use the training sessions to reinforce what they have learned

That is enough theory crafting. The fun begins in the next chapter where we will be going over basic games to prep your dog for more complex games down the line.

Chapter 4: Basic Games

"Dog training is a never-ending process of evolving."

– Ivan Balabanov

Let's start off with something simple. By simple, I mean that we are using games that require your dog to do something that comes naturally to them such as sniffing. From there, we can make small alterations and help us establish a foundation for more complex maneuvers in later chapters.

Clicker

This is not a game per se, but I highly recommend you familiarize your dog with a clicker first to make the training process a lot easier down the line.

A clicker is a powerful tool in dog training. It makes it easy to nail your timing. This little boxlike gadget holds a flat metal strip that makes a clear "click" sound when you press it with your thumb. This sound is clear and curt so that your dog can easily distinguish it from other noises.

Although you can say "good boy" or other praise to help your dog in training, the clicker makes everything more convenient. You can use it to tell your dog that they did something right without saying anything. Eventually, your dog will get used to the sound and will keep an ear out for this sound during training or play.

The idea is that you use the clicker to mark an event for your dog. For the timing, you click immediately when your dog does what you want and give them a treat right after. This helps your dog associate the click with the treat. They will know that they did something right when they hear that click, and they expect rewards to follow.

I highly recommend that at first, you keep plenty of treats ready. The goal is twofold. First is to give your dog the treat when they follow your command. You use rewards to reinforce desirable behavior and lack thereof to discourage undesirable behavior. This is called positive reinforcement. The second goal is to get your dog to believe that when they hear the click, some sort of reward is coming their way.

Of course, at some point, you need to wean your dog off the treats and start giving away rewards intermittently. After a week or two of using the clicker is a good time to space out the rewards. My advice here is to do it slowly. At first, reward once every 2 clicks, then 3, and so on. Then, you can randomize the intervals. That way, your dog assumes that as long as they keep doing what you ask, they will get their treats.

Objective

At the end of this training, your dog will learn that they will get a treat when they hear the click.

Application

When your dog makes the connection between the click and the treat, you can use it to mark desirable behavior when you are training them. This is particularly useful when you want your dog to perform a complex trick or games that have to be taught in many stages.

Just keep in mind that you will be using the clicker forever. You need to keep reminding your dog that the click means a reward.

Training Steps

The goal is to teach your dog that the click means that they did something right and that they are getting a reward for being a good boy. At this stage, you are not asking your dog to do anything. You are just introducing your dog to the sound. Here is a step-by-step breakdown:

- Wait until things are quiet and your dog is not busy with anything. Have plenty of treats ready, preferably their favorite treat.
- Click the clicker and immediately give your dog a treat. At first, your dog might be startled by the sound but they should calm down when given the treat.

- Click the clicker again and give your dog another treat. Now, your dog might start to put 2 and 2 together and associate the sound with the treat. They may look up and approach you, which is nice, but that behavior is not required. We are not rewarding the dog for doing anything other than to listen.
- Rinse and repeat for a few minutes before ending the training session. Continue with this training every day without doing anything different. Just click and treat until your dog clearly associates the click with the treat. At some point, the click will get your dog's attention immediately and then you know you have succeeded.
- From there, you can incorporate the clicker into things that your dog already learns to do. For example, if your dog knows the "sit" command already, instead of saying "good boy", you can just click and reward immediately.

The clicker is handy because it is distinctive. Again, a dog reads body language better so if you have to use verbal/auditory cues, you want to keep it nice and short so as not to confuse your pup. A clicker does just that.

Plus, you can accurately and quickly tell your dog that they did something right, assuming that you mastered the timing. Ideally, you need to do it within a second of your dog's action. Not before they perform the action and not after.

The problem with using verbal cues such as "good boy" or "good" is that we also use those words in everyday conversation. Yes, dogs can distinguish based on context, but you want to make it as easy as possible for them to learn. The click is distinct and not a sound your dog hears every day, making the clicker the perfect event market.

Potential Issue

If your dog is jumpy and gets frightened by strange noises, consider getting a quiet or adjustable clicker. When you go out and buy a clicker, test all of them if you can. Each one makes a different noise at a different volume.

When using a clicker with jumpy dogs, make sure to hold it behind your back instead of pointing it at your dog like pointing a remote at a TV. The strange object might startle them as well. Eventually, they will grow accustomed to the noise and you can use the clicker as normal.

Tag the Target

Let's play a quick game between us first. If I ask you where you put your phone, how would you answer it? If it is out of sight, you would probably say that it is in your bag or something. But if it is on the table 3 feet from you, you would point at it, right?

We usually point at things to identify them. Your dogs do not use their paws the same way. They may identify an object by pawing at it or using their nose.

When we think about targets, we might envision a dart board or something similar. A dog does not understand what a target is, but you can teach them that it is something that they can identify when you ask them.

So, your prop then is a target that you can buy online. It is a colorful object so your dog should recognize it quite easily. Alternatively, you can use a plastic lid from a small food package which is more durable than a paper target. Whatever you use, stick to it until your dog understands what you are asking them to do.

Objective

At the end of this training, your dog will learn to focus on a single object and learn to perform 2 actions with it when asked.

Application

This exercise, though simple to you, requires your dog to concentrate. Other than that, this exercise serves as a foundation for more complex games and tricks that require your dog to push things around.

Training Steps

The game is very simple. You ask your dog to touch the target with their nose. Dogs are curious creatures so when you show them the prop, their first instinct would be to sniff it.

If your dog does not seem interested, you can try to entice them by applying liver paste or making it smell of food somehow. When your dog learns to touch the target with their nose, you can then ask them to touch it using their paw.

Although you can mark the behavior with your voice, it is going to be more convenient to use a clicker. Here is the rundown of this game:

- Hold the prop in your hand and call your dog. They might become curious and immediately go to the prop and sniff it.
- If so, say "Tap" when your dog does that and click.
- If not, try to encourage your dog by tapping the prop with your finger. Your dog might now approach the prob to see what is so interesting. If they still do not stick their nose in, tap the prop again.
- After a while, your dog should come up to the prop and sniff it whenever you say "Tap". Then, you can move on to asking them to touch it with their paw but using a different command.
- Call your dog and say "Tap". They should go up and sniff the prop again. Then, tap it and say "Paw".
- Expect your dog to be confused the first time around. If so, put the prop in your hand and put a treat on top of it and hold your palm just high enough that your dog has to hook their paw to try and get it.

- When they do, say “paw” and click.
- Rinse and repeat until your dog learns to touch the prop with their paw whenever you say “paw”, occasionally asking them to “tap” it with their nose.
- Continue to do this until your dog is fluent in both commands.

Locate the Target

When your dog learned to touch and paw the target, you can take it a step further. The next step is to ask your dog to find the target in different places each time.

You do not have to lay the prop flat on the floor. You can also slap it on a vertical surface such as a door or a piece of furniture. Adding verticality is going to make the game extra challenging for your pup.

Objective

At the end of this training, your dog will learn how to perform a three-stage activity – “Go look”, “tap”, and “paw”.

Application

It is a simple game that gets your dog to really think about what they need to do. There are three different steps here, to look, find, and touch. This is one of those games that most dogs find mentally tiring, so it is a good option on a rainy day when going for a walk is out of the question.

Training Steps

This game is basically hide-and-seek and you need to go with your dog while they look around the house for the prop in the first few sessions. But when they understand what they need to do, they should be motivated enough to go look for the prop by themselves.

Here is how you play Locate the Target:

- Put the target or prop somewhere out of sight in a room. For your first session, put it somewhere obvious. You want your dog to learn that they need to find the target/prop first before you can hide them in more difficult locations.
- Use a cue like "Go look!" to initiate the game. 9 times out of 10, your dog will not know what you want them to do. So, lead them to the target and ask them to "tap" the prop. When they do, click and give them a treat.
- Rinse and repeat a few times throughout the session. You can move the prop around a little bit every game, but keep it easy for the first couple of sessions.
- Once your dog gets the hang of the game and can find the target wherever you put it, you can then ask your dog to "paw" in addition to "tap" the target.

Potential Issue

Sometimes, your dog may get bored or show signs that

they are not as enthusiastic about the game. If so, try to incentivize them by rubbing the target or prop with something that smells lovely to a dog such as liver paste.

Take It

Dogs only have one way to carry something: with their mouth. Set your dog up for success by choosing a toy wisely. It needs to be small enough to be held in a dog's mouth and something that your dog likes (but is not obsessed with) as well.

The best toy to train with is often the one that you can use to lay a game with right after. A squeaky toy is a good option here. Although you are teaching your dog to take things from your hand first, the ultimate goal is to get your dog to pick things up from the floor.

Objective

At the end of this training, your dog will learn how to take and hold something in their mouth. Another benefit here is that they learn to trust you enough to take things from you.

Application

This is a great exercise that is important for other tricks that involve your dog moving an item around. Your dog needs to master this exercise first before moving on to more complex exercises that really turn the gears inside your dog's head.

Training Steps

The biggest challenge to this exercise is that it is going to be difficult to use treats or a clicker. Your hands will be occupied and so is your dog's mouth. Hence, the toy must be good enough to incentivize your dog to pick it up.

That said, timing your cues is going to be important as usual. You need to say the command the second your dog picks up the toy.

With that in mind, here is a play-by-play breakdown:

- Select the object that your dog likes and can hold in their mouth. Take it and hold it in front of them.
- Try to make it interesting for your dog. For instance, if it is a squeaky toy, make it squeak. Otherwise, try waving it around a bit. You can also provide exciting commentary like "Look at it!" or "What is this?" until your dog takes notice and shows an interest.
- When your dog approaches the toy, hold it out and offer it to them. If they take it in their mouth, say "Take It". If your dog manages to get a firm grip on it, praise them.
- You can take the opportunity to reinforce this command when you and your dog are about to head outside to play. You can stop by their toy or pick one up, offer it to your dog, and say "Take It". If your dog interprets it as a sign that you want to play, they will pick up the toy happily.

Potential Issues

Some dogs will pick things up just because they like carrying things. Some are "mouth shy". Though dogs use their nose and mouth to explore the world, the idea of taking something from your hand on command is foreign to them.

Studies show that nervous dogs do not like having their mouths occupied if they are unsure of what is happening around them. It makes your dog feel vulnerable since your dog's first and last line of defense is their mouth (specifically, their teeth). So, when you ask them to hold onto things with their mouth, you are effectively disarming them, which explains why some dogs would be apprehensive about this.

If your dog is mouth-shy, take things slow. Praise your dog frequently and warmly, and take the small wins if your dog can hold onto the toy for a second or two. After a few sessions, your dog may learn that you are playing a harmless game and will be more comfortable holding things with their mouth.

Find the Treat

This is a very simple game that involves you hiding a treat in one hand and your dog has to point out where it is. Pretty self-explanatory, though the game here requires your dog to use their paw to point. This game does not require anything special. You only need a few treats.

Objective

At the end of this training, your dog will learn that patience is a virtue. It is better than force if they want something, at least from a human.

Application

This is a quick and fun activity you can do pretty much everywhere.

Training Steps

Here is a step-by-step breakdown:

- Hide a treat in one hand. It should be something that has a strong smell to help your dog figure out where the treat is.
- Kneel in front of your dog and order them to sit.
- Clench your fists and hold them out in front of your dog. Make sure you keep them close to the ground.
- Your dog's first instinct will be to sniff your hands. They will figure out fairly quickly which hand the treat is in.
- Your dog's first instinct will also be to try and pry your hands open with their mouth. If so, say "No" firmly and pull your hand back slightly.
- It will take a while for your dog to figure out what they need to do. Be patient.
- If your dog is clearly confused, use your free hand to gently tap their paw.
- Some dogs can put 2 and 2 together and realize that

if they cannot use their mouths, they should try to use their paws.

- When your dog finally figures that they need to use their paw, you can put your hands back on the floor. They will paw the hand with the treat. If so, let them do it for a few seconds. Chances are that they are exerting some amount of force on your hand to get it open. If so, say "Gently" in a low and soft tone. It will cause your dog to stop for a second.
- The goal here is to get your dog to gently touch your hand with their paw, not trying to pry it open. The moment your dog rests their paw on your hand lightly, even for a second, reveal the treat immediately and give it to them.
- Rinse and repeat a few times every day for a week or so. Your dog will eventually learn that they just need to touch your hand with their paw to get to the treat.

3 Cups 1 Treat

Yes, the kids' game of 3 Cups and 1 Ball can be used as a dog brain teaser as well, except we will use treats instead. This is an easier alternative to the Treat Hunting game I mentioned before because it does not take as much time to set up and it works well with small dogs.

Objective

At the end of this training, your dog will learn how to use

their senses and dexterity to solve a problem.

Application

This simple game can keep them engaged and it is rewarding for them.

Training Steps

The simplest variation of this game does not require you to say anything. Your dog should be enticed by the smell of the treat and will go look for it on their own. Once your dog learns the basics of the game, you can make it a bit more challenging. Here's a step-by-step breakdown:

- Prepare 3 plastic cups. Make sure that your dog is present and watching.
- First, put treats under all 3 cups and back up and encourage your dog to come and find the treats.
- Your dog will know where the treats are. They will also know that they need to push the cups over to get to the treat. This is easier said than done because they need to tip the cups over somehow.
- Give them a few minutes. If they are still struggling, give them a hand and see if they can flip other cups over.
- Rinse and repeat a few times until your dog learns to topple the cups.
- For the next game, you can put one treat under one cup and shuffle in front of your dog and let them figure out which one has the treat.

Search and Munch

This is another variation of a treat hunting game. This time, the treats are all consolidated in one place. All your dog has to do is to get to it, and therein lies the challenge. This is one of my favorite activities that involve simple household props that makes the game challenging but also rewarding for your dog.

Objective

At the end of this training, your dog will learn how to use their dexterity and ingenuity, and to work in stages.

Application

Complex puzzles will better engage your dog. If the game is too easy, your dog will grow bored of it since it requires very little effort to solve.

Training Steps

You will need a muffin pan and tennis balls for this game. Ideally, the muffin pan has 9 or 12 slots. Ensure you have enough tennis balls for this. Here's how to play this game:

- Make sure that your dog is present and aware of what you are doing
- Put a treat into every cup inside the pan and place a tennis ball on it
- Put the pan down and let your dog figure out the game.

- Your dog will obviously smell the treat and try to get to it. But they will soon realize that it is not as simple as pushing the balls aside because it is impossible.
- Your dog has to lift each ball to get to the treat because the cups are deep, making pushing not a viable option.
- Once your dog figures it out, they will go through each cup until they get all the treats. You can sit back and record a video of it to show your friends and family how smart your dog is!

Note

As you can probably tell, although these brain teaser games will put your dog's wit to the test, they are still relatively simple in design. You can buy such treat-finding puzzles which will be far more challenging but still engaging for your dog.

I highly recommend you invest in one if your dog is a persistent treat hunter. It will keep your dog busy on a rainy day as it is designed to be far more complex than puzzles made with household items.

Check the local pet stores. They will have a few of these in stock and one or two on display so you can try and see if it is something you want. Some of these will require your dog to use directional pressure to get to the treat. Others may require your dog to move a few blocks out of the way or push a lever to get to the treat.

Fetch

A simple game of fetch that no dog could hate, though some dogs need a bit of encouragement.

Objective

At the end of this training, your dog will learn how to use their agility to pick up the ball and rehearse "come" and "drop it".

Application

This exercise is a great workout for your dog.

Training Steps

Your dog needs to learn how to "Drop It" and "Come" first. You also need an appropriately-sized ball. Unless your dog is very small, then a tennis ball will be enough. You do need a larger, softer ball if your dog is a giant breed. The idea is that the object should be small enough for dogs to carry in their mouths easily.

When you have the right toy for the job, here's how to play fetch:

- Start by bringing your dog to the backyard or a relatively small room.
- Grab your dog's attention by playing with the ball. Toss it into the air, bounce it off the ground, etc. until your dog looks at you.
- Then, throw the ball. Do not throw it too far. Point to it and say "fetch". Your dog should run after it and pick it up. When they do, say "Come".
- Your dog may come to you or at least look at you. If the latter, say "come" only one more time. When your dog starts to walk to you, get down on your knees.
- When they are close, tell your dog to "drop it" instead of trying to take it from your dog's mouth. Praise and reward your dog with a treat then take the ball and play with it for a bit, making the ball look enticing before throwing it again.

Potential Issue

Sometimes, your dog might not be interested in the ball. One cause of this is that they lack the "drive" to chase after the ball. If that is the case, you can try to increase their drive by using a different toy.

You can use the rope for the tug-of-war game with your dog for the job. In this case, play a short game of tug-of-war first before throwing it and saying "fetch". Your dog should have enough drive after the first game and chase after it. Once your dog is familiar with "fetch", you can try swapping between the ball and rope or just use the rope to play fetch.

Key Takeaway

In this chapter, we looked at some basic exercises. These are fairly simple in the sense that they do not involve many commands. They are simple extensions of things that your dogs are doing naturally. Here's a short recap of the exercises we covered in this chapter:

- Clicker: Used to mark desirable behavior, making it easier to train your dog later on.
- Tag the target: Requires your dog to interact with the target or prop of your choice, useful for more advanced tricks that require your dog to push something.
- Locate the target: Though simple, this exercise is intended to teach your dog how to tackle a task in stages, which prepares them for more challenging

tricks.

- Take it: A simple trick that requires your dog to hold onto something for you, handy for future exercises that involve this action.
- Find the treat: Challenges your dog to find the treat using their keen sense of smell.
- 3 cups, 1 treat: Similar to the previous exercise, but with a fun twist.
- Search and munch: Similar to the previous exercise, but your dog has to perform a fairly complex maneuver to get to the treat.
- Fetch: Simple and fun game to play in between mind-teaser games.

In the next chapter, we will go over more difficult but also more fun and engaging activities for your dog.

Chapter 5: Intermediate Games

"Stubborn is a good thing. If they are doing the wrong thing they are stubborn. If they are doing the right thing they are 'committed' ... just get them stubborn on the right thing."

– Chad Mackin

In this chapter, we will go over exercises that are a bit harder but should not be too challenging for your dog. With a bit of patience and repetition, you can teach your dog how to play these games the way they are meant to be played.

Tug-of-War

The classic game of tug. You need a tug toy or soft rope for the job. This is a good activity to do between mental exercises to bring your dog's energy level right back up.

Objective

At the end of this training, your dog will learn how to have fun but in a controlled manner.

Application

This is a building block to another activity where you ask your dog to open the door. This is also a good exercise to teach/reinforce the "drop it" command.

Training Steps

The training would be smoother if your dog learns the "Drop It" command, but it is optional. Here's how to play tug-of-war:

- First, present the toy to your dog. Wiggle it a bit. When they look at it, click and reward.
- Your dog should be interested in the toy now. When they start to mouth it, say "Grab". They may pull it out of your hand, and that is okay. Only hold onto it lightly for now.
- When your dog pulls the rope out of your hand, click and reward generously.
- When your dog is confident in pulling the rope from your hand, the game can now begin. This time, hold the rope tightly. When your dog pulls, add some resistance and pull back, saying "Tug" when you do so. Every time you pull, say "tug" in an enthusiastic voice. Your dog will pull in response.
- When you are ready, ask your dog to "drop it", assuming your dog understands that command already.
- If not, lure your dog with a second toy to get them to drop the first one. When your dog goes after the second toy, pick up the first one and the game can begin again.

- At first, you can say “drop it” the second your dog drops the toy. In subsequent sessions, say the command earlier so that your dog understands what they need to do.

Potential Issue

Sometimes, your dog becomes overexcited and does not want to let go. If so, try to entice them to do so by showing them their favorite treat at eye level so you can retrieve the toy safely.

In some cases, your dog is stubborn and continues to hold onto the toy or runs away with it. If so, do not go after your dog. Disengage and set up another training or just end the session then and there.

Handshake

Though an optional activity for your dog, it is still a fun activity. Think of this exercise as teaching them how to greet other people using human language.

Objective

At the end of this training, your dog will learn how to greet other people using human gestures, but more importantly to build trust. More on that in a moment.

Application

If your dog has a habit of jumping on you when they see you, you can use this command to remind them how to greet you properly. Most importantly, this command is useful for dogs that are "paw shy".

You see, dogs are sensitive about their paws. Don't believe me? Try to grab your dog's paw and they will immediately retract it the second you touch it. Some dogs are even more sensitive about others touching their paws.

So, this exercise helps your dog get comfortable with people touching their paws. This is especially useful at the groomer when they need to trim your dog's nails.

Also, your dog also has a dominant paw the same way we have a dominant hand. If you spend an hour or two watching your dog, you will notice that your dog usually leads with one paw over the other. This is their dominant paw and you should use that paw when teaching your dog this trick.

Training Steps

Your dog needs to know the "Sit" command first. Here's how to teach your dog how to shake hands:

- Ask your dog to "sit", then treat.
- When your dog sits, try touching his upper leg on the side of the leading paw. Your dog should lift their paw by instinct.
- Regardless, carefully slip your hand under your dog's paw and hold it gently. Say "Shake" when you do.
- Hold your dog's paw for only 1-2 seconds, shaking it gently, and offer your dog a treat with your other

hand.

- Make sure that you do not close your hand around your dog's paw. They may feel trapped if you do.
- Rinse and repeat until your dog learns to give their paw when you say "Shake" without you needing to touch them first.

Follow the Scent

Dogs have an incredibly sensitive nose. They use their sense of smell more than others. You can use that to create an engaging game for your dog.

Objective

At the end of this training, your dog will learn how to trust their instinct and ingenuity to work toward something rewarding.

Application

This is a fun activity more than anything. Considering that your dog uses their sense of smell the most, you are missing out if you do not have a couple of games that are centered on this sense. This activity also satisfies your dog's need to use their nose.

Training Steps

The goal of this game is to put down a scent trail that your dog can follow to their reward. You need to plan this in advance because you have around 15 minutes before the scent becomes too faint that your dog could not detect it.

Another thing to keep in mind is that it is better to play this game outdoors because it might get messy. Here's what you need to do:

- Prepare a bag with smelly content that is appealing to your dog. Leftovers, a chicken carcass slathered in broth, or ground meat are all good options. The broth is a must so that it would drip down, leaving behind a trail of scent.
- Whatever you choose, wrap it in a piece of cheesecloth or any fabric that you can find and tie a string to it so you can pull it around.
- Put the bag down on the ground and pull it around. Try to cover as much area as possible so your dog does not get to the end too soon. Although you can meander around, do not cross over the path you have laid down. Try to leave a clear trail behind you.
- When you are satisfied with your trail, pick up the bag and put it in a plastic bag. The trail has a clear end and the content of the bag is not the reward.
- If you want, you can put some treats there under a cup that your dog has to overcome. You can also put the cardboard box or even the puzzle you bought from the pet store here as the final challenge for your dog.
- To begin the game, take your dog to the start of the

scent trail. Most dogs will pick up the scent and start sniffing right away. If not, you can put a small piece of treat to get them going.

- Follow your dog as they follow the scent. Try to encourage them back onto the track if your dog becomes distracted.
- When your dog gets the hang of the game, you can use subtler scents. You can just use meat or fish without the broth. It is going to be more challenging, but your dog should be able to follow the scent regardless.

Dog Whisperer

Did you know that when you are talking to people and suddenly drop your volume to a whisper, the other person is likely to whisper as well? When you suddenly go quiet, others start to pay more attention to you.

Dogs can hear better than us and they are used to hearing loud noises. So, you can surprise your dog by being quiet.

Objective

At the end of this training, your dog will learn that routines can have their surprises and it is worth paying attention. When you do not voice your cues loudly, your dog will pay more attention to your body language to help them figure out what you want them to do.

Application

The idea is to get your dog to pay more attention in training. That said, this exercise should not be used during exercises that your dog is not familiar with. They need all the help they can get at that stage. Stick to playing this game with activities your dog knows well as it can be effective in reinforcing the knowledge.

Note

Some dogs may get nervous when playing this game. If your dog appears to be nervous instead of curious, stop the game and use verbal cues as normal.

Training Steps

This activity requires you to go through activities that your dog is already familiar with, but in a whisper. Here's how it's done:

- Pick one session to do this exercise and think of a few exercises that your dog is already familiar with such as "Sit", "Come", etc.
- Have plenty of treats ready and go through the exercise as normal, except the verbal cues you give are quieter than usual. Make sure to be a bit more generous with the treats this time.

Hide-and-Seek

A simple and fun game of hide-and-seek that you can play with your dog. For the best results, consider having someone else play with your dog to distract them while you go and hide. Afterwards, they and the other person can go look for you together.

Objective

At the end of this training, your dog will learn how to use their nose and ear to find you.

Application

This is a fun way to reinforce the "Come" command. You also reinforce the idea that you are someone worth looking for.

Training Steps

The goal is to get your dog to find you. The first couple of times, they will need human assistance to guide and help them understand the game. The goal is to teach your dog to play this game without a human cheerleader. Here's how you play hide-and-seek:

- Have your friend or family member distract your dog and you go hide. At first, you can just go and stand in the other room. You can make the game more difficult later on.
- Let your friend know beforehand that they need to build up excitement for the game while they wait with the dog. They can count to 10 loudly and then say "Coming!"
- The game begins. Your friend's job is to help your dog look for you by providing commentary and encouragement in an excited tone. What they say

does not matter. What matters is the tone that encourages your dog to go look for you.
- Drop hints by saying your dog's name and "Come". Your dog should hear the command and go to you.
- When your dog finds you, praise and reward with a treat. Give them a lot of love before playing 1-2 more times.

Notes

A few things to mention here. One, you can also hold your dog's favorite treat in your hand as you walk out of the room so as to leave behind a faint scent for your dog to follow.

Also, a game of hide-and-seek should not be longer than 60 seconds. Anything more than that and your dog might start to lose interest.

Verticality makes the game a lot more challenging for your dog because they usually do not look up. Consider this when you want to make the game more interesting for your pup.

Surprisingly, hiding right behind an open door is also good because it encourages your dog to be thorough with their search. From your scent and voice, they know that you are there, but they have to navigate around the door to find you, and it might take them a while to figure it out.

Indoor Digging

This game builds upon your dog's instinct to dig. Although this behavior is annoying, there is little you can do other than control it. This exercise is one way to do this.

Dogs need to dig. Some breeds are wired to dig such as Dachshunds because they were bred to hunt prey. Other dogs go through a phase and can grow out of it. Regardless, you can get this out of your dog's system by creating an area where they can dig.

Objective

At the end of this training, your dog will learn how to use their dexterity and intuition to navigate to the treat, to trust their nose to guide them to the goodies, and that the box is one place you are okay with them digging.

Application

This game is the perfect option to keep your dog occupied on a rainy day. It also helps you control your dog's digging habit as well. You can also make the game more interesting by piling on the cardboard and papers and adding treats at different depths.

Yes, you will have to clean up after your dog if they dig too hard, but at least you can reuse all of that scraps for subsequent games and give your dog hours of fun.

Training Steps

You will need a box for this game. The cardboard boxes

that you have from your office will do. Just make sure that there are no tapes or staples that can harm your dog. The box also needs to be short enough so that your dog can get in and out easily. Here's what you need to do:

- Start with an empty box and let your dog inspect it. You just want them to realize that the box is there first.
- Then, you can try to encourage them to go into the box. Put a treat just out of reach so that your dog has to take their first step in.
- Do not pick your dog up and lift them in. Be patient and let your dog climb in on their own. This is also an opportunity for your dog to think for themselves.
- Then, put another treat in the center to encourage your dog to move in further.
- Now, you can start the game. You can put a few more treats in there and use an old towel or scrunched-up pieces of paper or pieces of cardboard to cover them. Then, encourage your dog to get in there and find the treat. They should already smell the treat and start rummaging around by themselves.

Treat Hunting

As you can guess by the name, this exercise is treasure hunting. This exercise is a great activity between serious training exercises. Limit the play area to a single room.

This room needs to be separate from the training area because when the training session is complete, you will take your dog there.

This activity is fun and rewarding for your dog. For one, you can use this to reward your dog instead of handing them a treat directly. Remember the treat jackpot tip I gave you previously? You apply that in this game. Also, your dog will think that this game is pure reward and they can get a lot of delicious treats if they follow their nose.

Objective

At the end of this training, your dog will learn how to be more alert and use their keen nose to sniff out treats and figure things out on their own. They will also learn to look forward to this activity because it involves plenty of treats.

Application

Indulgent exercises and brain teasers offer better results overall because you are engaging in different kinds of activities. While your dog's "thinking muscles" are tired from the brain teaser activity, a quick and fun exercise can give your dog the energy boost they need. Plus, giving your dog unexpected fun like this also reminds your dog that you provide them with a lot of things they love and this reinforces your relationships.

Training Steps

Prepare the room before you start your daily training session. Hide treats in many different locations, from obvious to obscure, to make the game interesting for your dog.

Since dogs will start by sniffing the floor, leave some treats under the corner of a rug, by the feet of furniture, etc. Since dogs are unlikely to look above their head when they are trying to find something, be careful about placing things higher than your dog's eye level.

You can leave a treat on a chair, behind a cushion, etc. Only place a few that are high up that your dog can get to, but will require a bit of effort on their part.

Here's what you need to do:

- Have a dozen treats ready and hide them throughout the room. Put only 3 treats at most in hard-to-get-to corners. After you have hidden all the goodies, leave and shut the door.
- Train your dog as you would normally.
- After you have completed the first difficult exercise, head straight to the door of the treasure room and make sure your dog follows you. Say "Go look!" in an enthusiastic tone.
- Your dog may be confused the first time around, so guide them to their first and easiest-to-find treat. Keep the momentum by cheering for your dog to find the rest. You can say something like "Find the treat!", or "Where is it?" to keep the energy up.

- Your dog will most likely sniff out the treats on the floor without too much issue but the game becomes interesting when verticality is involved.
- Just like the first treat, you can show your dog where one of them is and encourage them to find the rest.
- When your dog has found all the treats, they should be happy and full of energy again. Use that to your advantage and move back to the difficult exercise right after. Your dog will perform better because the game gives your dog the energy and enthusiasm to interact with you.

Bar Hop

A simple exercise where you ask your dog to jump over a bar. Safety will be your #1 priority here. Although it is tempting to see how high your dog can jump, it can quickly lead to injuries.

This exercise is not suitable for dogs with orthopedic issues such as hip dysplasia or partial dislocation of joints. Also, if your dog is not fully grown (around 18 months or younger), then do not have your dog jump any higher than elbow height.

But if you want some numbers to compare, the highest that agility competitions will go is 24 inches. Getting over 50 is impressive and 60 is very rare. The highest record was made on 14 September 2017 by a very good girl named Feather, a greyhound, who leaped over 75.5

inches.

Should you go for that number? I cannot recommend it, but if you want your dog to take part in agility competitions, work toward 24 inches, but it might be impossible depending on your dog's size. Regardless, start small and work your way up, and do not push your dog to jump any higher than they are comfortable.

Objective

At the end of this training, your dog will learn how to build confidence in jumping over high obstacles.

Application

This is a great exercise to implement between mind teaser games as it allows your dog to stretch and hop around a bit. It is also one of the first tricks your dog needs to learn to join an agility competition.

Training Steps

You need to set up a jump bar. I recommend you get a lightweight plastic jump bar that falls easily when your dog hits it. But two stacks of books and a plastic pipe will also do just fine. With the bar set, here's how to play Bar Hop:

- Set the bar as low as you can and walk over with your dog. You can use a leash to lead your dog over for now. Yes, it is very easy but you want your dog to be familiar with going over the bar.

- Rinse and repeat a few times and as the dog goes over the bar, say "hop", then click and give your dog a treat.
- Take off the leash and your dog to sit on one side of the bar. Then, you can walk over the bar and ask your dog to "come" to you.
- When your dog walks over the bar, say "hop" again. Rinse and repeat a few times and try to switch sides.
- Now, you can raise the bar. For adult dogs, you can raise an inch at a time. For smaller or young dogs, use smaller increments. Repeat the exercise until the bar is up to the elbow.
- Your dog might knock the bar over a few times but reward them anyway. You want your dog to build muscle memory and like the activity.
- Now you can introduce the visual cue. Stand close to your dog and, with a flat palm, sweep your arm over the bar and say "hop". If your dog needs some help, you can toss a treat over the bar as you perform the visual cue and say "send".
- Rinse and repeat until your dog learns to do it without much help.

Potential Issues

Some dogs might cheat by circling around the bar. Although you have to commend their intelligence, they still need to learn the jump. To stop that, you can put one side of the bar against the wall and stand on the opposite end to stop your dog from going around. Alternatively, you can put up chairs to block them.

That said, it is also possible that your dog is uncertain, injured, or does not want to jump at all. In any case, only try to do this a few times and if your dog still is not interested, you can switch to other activities.

Key Takeaway

In this chapter, we looked at some tricky exercises that build upon previous training covered in this and my other book. With a bit of practice, your dog should be able to play these games without an issue. Here's a short recap of the exercises we covered in this chapter:

- Tug-of-war: Teaches your dog the importance of controlled play.
- Handshake: Gets your dog used to having their paws touched.
- Follow the scent: Challenges your dog to use their sense of smell to track down a target.
- Dog whisperer: Challenges your dog to listen carefully and rely on your body language for guidance.
- Hide and seek: Challenges your dog to navigate the house to find you, using their sense of smell and hearing.
- Indoor digging: A fun alternative to your dog digging your backyard.
- Treat hunting: Challenges your dog to find hidden

treats hidden throughout the room and using their sense of smell.

- Bar hop: A fun exercise to get your dog comfortable with going airborne.

In the next chapter, we will go over some challenging tricks you can teach your dog.

Chapter 6: Advanced Games

"Always challenge, never overwhelm."

– Chad Mackin

For the final chapter, we will go over challenging games and activities that require your dog to perform complex actions that may not come to them naturally. These activities build upon other exercises and commands and require your dog to perform activities in a chain.

Balance the Treat

You have probably seen videos where a dog delicately balanced a treat on their cute nose and then flip and chomp on it on command. Does it look cool? Yes. Does it take a long time to teach your dog this trick? Absolutely.

It looks simple to you, but this is very difficult for your dog to pull off. They need to be agile enough to balance the treat and understand that they need to do that until told. The training involves several steps over the course of weeks if not months.

So instead, I will tell you a variation of this game that does not involve complex choreography.

Objective

At the end of this training, your dog will learn that they need your permission to take what they want.

Application

It is never a bad idea to teach your dog activities that instill discipline. This exercise reinforces the idea that your dog needs your permission to do something. Plus, you also get to rehearse the "Leave It" and "Take It" commands as well.

Training Steps

The goal is to teach your dog to balance the treat on their paw and eat it only when you tell them to. For this activity to work, your dog needs to understand the "Leave It" and "Take It" commands.

Here's how to do it:

- Make sure your dog is lying down with their paws in front of them, or use the "Down" command.
- Put the treat on your dog's paw. Your dog's first instinct would be to go for the treat. If so, say "Leave it".
- Some dogs are disciplined and know you well enough to know that you're not the kind to be dropping treats like this, so they will look to you for guidance.
- Regardless, only wait a few seconds before giving your dog the "Take it" cue.
- Some dogs will take the cue and eat the treat. If

your dog is still hesitant, you can pick up the treat and give it to them. Say "take it" one more time. Do not say it a third time because that will confuse them.

Note

It is better to teach this trick when your dog is laying down because they would be most comfortable in that position and do not have to worry too much about balancing the treat.

Thanks to how a dog's paws are shaped, your dog does not have to focus too much on trying to balance the treat. It is much more difficult to balance a treat on the nose.

Hoop Jump

This exercise involves your dog jumping through a hoop instead of over a bar. As always, safety is your #1 concern here. A toy hula hoop will suffice. If you use a clicker, you can hold it and the hoop because you need the other hand to give a visual cue.

Objective

At the end of this training, your dog will learn how to use their dexterity to overcome an obstacle.

Application

In terms of simplicity, setting up a hoop jump is easier than a bar jump because you only need a hoop. This is a fun game to play with your dog between training exercises and on a rainy day when you cannot take your dog outside.

Training Steps

- Position you, your dog, and the hoop. Start by setting the hoop to the ground first. If you hold the hoop with your left hand, hold the treat in your right, and your dog should sit on the left. Do the opposite if you prefer using your left hand.
- Lure your dog through the hoop with the treat. When your dog's paw passes through the hoop, toss the treat a short distance to guide your dog all the way through. When your dog goes after the treat, turn around and do it again. Rinse and repeat a few times so your dog is familiar with the hoop.
- Then, you can add a visual and verbal cue. Shake the hoop to indicate that you want your dog to go through. Lure your dog in as normal but say "hoop" before you toss the treat.
- Rinse and repeat a few times, phasing out the treat as you go.
- Now, you can raise the hoop bit by bit at each repetition, but do not go any higher than your dog's stomach. At the same time, position the hoop further and further away from your dog. If they need encouragement, you can use treats for now.
- If your dog is a healthy adult, you can raise the hoop even higher. You can also add another cue by

sweeping your hand down through the hoop.

Potential Issue

Sometimes, your dog can get hung up on the hoop and does not try to get out immediately. That is fine. Wait a bit and see if they can get themselves out. You can try to use a treat to encourage them to figure it out.

Do not keep your dog there for too long. Lower the hoop when they start to become nervous. If you wait too long, your dog might be afraid of the hoop and may not want to jump through it again.

Bring the Bowl

This exercise is a lesson in manners where your dog brings their bowl to you when mealtime comes around. It is best to do it before mealtime so that they have a stronger motivation to learn.

Just make sure that the bowl is something that your dog can pick up and hold easily. Do not use a metal or ceramic bowl as it will be too slippery or heavy to hold and your dog may drop it. Instead, use a light and sturdy molded plastic bowl that is small and in an appropriate shape.

Objective

At the end of this training, your dog will learn how to take the initiative and chain many actions together, and to get you to feed your dog (more on that in the next section).

Application

With several weeks of training, your dog should be fairly good at this game. They learn to be more independent and they might just bring their bowl to you unprompted when they know it is time for dinner.

Training Steps

The goal is to get your dog to bring you their empty bowl on command. Make sure your dog understands the prerequisite command "Take It" first before attempting this exercise. Just like "Locate the Target", this is a 3-step process.

For the first couple of sessions, you need to start by handing your dog the bowl. Eventually, they need to learn to go and collect it by themselves and bring it to you so you can give them food.

Here is the step-by-step rundown:

- For the first couple of weeks, play the "Take It" exercise using the bowl first. Ask them to take it from your hand and hold it for a few seconds.
- Try to encourage them to hold it for longer in the following sessions. At the end of each practice, you can take the bowl from your dog and feed them dinner. That way, your dog starts to associate holding the bowl with good things (food and treats).

- Your goal is to get your dog to hold the bowl for 5 seconds.
- From there, use the "Take It" command to get your dog to hold the bowl in their mouth, then try to get them to bring the bowl to the counter where you left their food.
- At this stage, you are teaching your dog to carry the bowl, so use the command "Carry" as your dog saunters over to the counter. Follow alongside them to the counter.
- Rinse and repeat these two steps until your dog learns to take the bowl from your hand and walks to the counter with minimal guidance on your part.
- For the third and final stage, your goal is to get your dog to look for the bowl and bring it to you. This is going to be the hardest part of the exercise so be patient. First, go with your dog to the area where the bowl is usually kept and ask them to "Take It" like they would from your hand. Ensure you position the bowl in a way that your dog can easily pick it up from a flat surface. The bowl might need a rim or handle for your dog to hold onto. When your dog picks it up, praise it happily and keep the momentum going by saying "Carry" and walking with them back to the counter. Afterwards, you can take the bowl from your dog when they are at the counter, fill it with food, and let them eat.
- When your dog learns to take the bowl from the floor and carry it to the counter reliably, you can try

to give a simple cue like nodding toward the bowl, instead of walking your dog to the bowl and saying "Take It" until your dog looks at it to signal that you want your dog to go and take the bowl and bring it to you. As they do so, say "Carry" to reinforce their behavior.

Potential Issues

Considering that this is a rather challenging exercise, you will need to make sure your dog could perform each action in each stage fairly well first before proceeding.

Remember that each training/play session should be short. So, if your dog struggles at any particular step for a while, consider calling it quits there. Your dog would probably be quite nervous at that point. Instead, ask them to repeat the previous step.

For example, the most challenging part of this exercise is the final stage where you ask your dog to pick up the bowl and bring it to the counter. If your dog fails to do so after 5 times or so, consider dropping back to the second stage where you just hand the bowl to your dog and ask them to carry it to the counter.

If your dog fails to even do that, go back to another step and ask your dog to just take the bowl from your hand with the "Take It" command. Just let them hold for a few seconds and then you can feed them.

On the off-chance that your dog gets so nervous that they even forget the first step, take the bowl, fill it with dog food, make sure they see you doing it in the process, and ask them to sit. If your dog is fluent with this command, they should sit and you can feed them. Otherwise, lure your dog into a sitting position and then feed them.

Do not feel bad about dropping back to the previous stages of the exercise like this. It happens sometimes. Your dog might just be overwhelmed because the training's pacing is too fast. You can try this again the next day.

Close the Door

In this exercise, you want your dog to close the door on cue. Dogs and doors do not really get along well. They are usually apprehensive when working with a moving door, so this exercise helps them build up confidence and you can ask them to close the door for you!

Objective

At the end of this training, your dog will learn how to use their dexterity to interact with a large moving object and perform a complex task.

Application

You can practice this exercise every time you walk through a door to build a habit for your dog. They close the door for you, which can be handy and will impress other people.

Training Steps

Your dog needs to understand the "Tag the Target" game first before you try this exercise. Here's how to do it:

- Put the target/prop on the door using tape at an appropriate height. It has to be tall enough that your dog cannot touch it with their nose, and has to stand up and put their weight on their paws to touch it. Make sure you put it away from the edge so that your dog does not pinch themselves when closing the door.
- Walk through the door and ask your dog to sit on the side where they have to push the door.
- First, keep the door closed and ask your dog to "paw" the target. Click and give your dog a treat. Consider putting the treat behind your dog so they have to turn around to "reset".
- Open the door by an inch and ask your dog to "paw" the target again. When your dog does so, pin a command. I use "Close door", click and treat.
- Rinse and repeat until your dog knows to close the door when you ask them to "close door" only. At every repetition, take a small step back and open the door another inch but stop before the door is too wide open. Your dog should still be leaning on the door when it is fully closed.
- Remove the target and ask your dog to "close door". Expect your dog to be confused here because they thought that they needed to push on the target.
- If so, close the door and ask your dog to "close

door" with the target present, but hold onto it this time. When your dog is just about to touch the target, pull it away. Click and reward your dog generously. Rinse and repeat as you slowly open the door with each repetition.

- The goal is to get your dog to push the door by themselves without you standing close to them, and without the target present.

Open the Door

If you teach your dog to close the door, it follows that you should teach them how to open one as well. Of course, this exercise only works with doors that do not have a latch. You can tape down the mechanism or leave doors slightly ajar.

Objective

At the end of this training, your dog will learn how to open doors marked with a rope.

Application

If you want, you can set up the training area with ropes on both sides of the door and tape the latch mechanism down. That way, you can ask your dog to open and close the door for you. However, the door must be a pull door from the outside.

Training Steps

Your dog needs to understand the game of tug-of-war first. If your dog is familiar with this game, then you can teach your dog to open the door by:

- First, have two lengths of rope. Tie one to the door so that it swings open easily when your dog pulls on the rope. The rope should be thick and have a knot at the end. As for the length, you just have to experiment and see which works best for your dog. Start with the rope tied lower first then work your way up.
- Play tug-of-war with your dog using the second length of rope. Tie the knot at the end the same way as the first. Your dog should associate the rope with pulling.
- After a game or two of tug, bring your dog to the door. Hold the first length of rope just above your dog's eye level. Say "tug" and see if your dog pulls on the rope as instructed. When they do, say "drop it", click and reward.
- Tie the rope higher up and hold it closer to the door in every repetition. Work your way slowly up and closer to the door until you eventually let go of the rope.
- Using the "tug" command, get your dog to approach the dangling rope and open the door by pulling the rope.

Key Takeaway

Finally, we covered some more challenging exercises that require your dog to perform complex maneuvers and/or do something that might not necessarily come to them naturally. It will take some time before your dog gets the hang of these exercises, but it is fun and rewarding in the long run. Here's a short recap of the exercises we covered in this chapter:

- Balance the treat: Instills discipline.
- Hoop jump: A building block to improving your dog's agility.
- Bring the bowl: Useful for your dog to tell you when they are hungry, and it is considered good etiquette.
- Close the door: Fun to look at, but also helps your dog build confidence around moving doors.
- Open the door: A good trick to impress your friends, but also helps your dog build confidence.

Conclusion

And there you have it, 20+ exercises to keep your dog well-entertained and far away from unwanted behavior. As you can tell, you do not need much to keep a dog happy. A lot of games you see in and beyond this book are, in a way, a different variation from children's games. This just goes on to reinforce the fact that dogs truly are fur babies.

No matter what games you play, safety should always be at the forefront of your thought. Active games are most effective in getting your dog to burn the extra energy, but they can get a little too excited and injure themselves.

So, even though you are having fun with your dog, keep an eye out for them and try not to get too excited yourself. When it comes to choosing the games to play, it is not so much about you, but rather about your dog. Their breed, size, age, and overall health determine what kind of games they can play.

For instance, a greyhound can play the hoop jump easily and you can set it pretty high, but the game is not suitable for chihuahuas.

You can use the dog categorization list in Chapter 2 to give you an idea of how your dog will behave. But keep in mind that every dog is different and will stray from the norm in one way or another. At the end of the day, it is up to you to observe your dog's behavior to have a good idea of their temperament and then choose appropriate games for them.

"Smart" dogs, though they are indeed cunning, can be a bit tricky to train. This is because they sort of care about what they are doing with you. It has to be entertaining for them to engage with you. Of course, all dogs love spending time with their humans, but it would be better if you are doing something fun for them.

On the flip side, dogs that just do as you ask are not "slow". It is a matter of preference. "Smart" dogs want to do something fun while others think that interacting with you is fun enough.

Some dogs are confident and take the initiative. I love working with them the most because they trust their instinct and they trust that you would guide them if they need help. They follow your instructions without hesitation and are willing to try something new and interesting. Count yourself lucky if your dog falls into this archetype.

Shy or timid dogs present a different kind of challenge. They are happy to interact with you but they are a bit apprehensive when it comes to doing new things, especially if it goes against their instincts such as asking them for a paw shake. For these dogs, take things slow and be patient.

Another archetype is not so much an archetype, but

something to be corrected. Obsessive behaviors can occur in dogs of all breeds. But the breeds can determine the source of obsession. Obsessive behaviors do not bring your dog joy. If anything, it makes your dog anxious and restless, so it is imperative that you address the problem immediately.

If your dog is obsessed with a certain toy, remove it when they are absent. When it comes to activity, put them through an energy-intensive exercise first and keep that activity short. Also, show your dog that you are willing to engage with them but are not very enthusiastic about it.

When it comes to training/playing, be precise about the timing, gesture, and tone that you use. Keep everything short and concise. Sometimes, your dog might get confused because you make some unintentional gesture or repeat the command many times. That's why you should keep everything simple, stay still, speak your commands and use gestures clearly.

So long as you do the above, you can teach your dog pretty much every trick under the sun. Just keep in mind that complex tricks have to be taught in stages and that it will take a while before your dog masters the trick.

With all that said, I have one final tip: Have fun!

~~$25~~ FREE BONUS

House Train Your New Pup Today!

Scan QR code above to claim your free bonus!

OR

visit bit.ly/vipdogbonus

Ready to Keep a Tidy House & A Happy Pup?

Inside this included ebook for new dog parents, you'll find:

- ✓ The simple way to housebreak any dog - guaranteed... even if they're disobedient at first!
- ✓ Guided instructions for both dog parents who are at home more, and busy parents who are unable to be home all day.
- ✓ How to identify your dog's natural temperament to accelerate the housebreaking process!

Scan QR code above to claim your free bonus!

OR

visit bit.ly/vipdogbonus

Made in the USA
Middletown, DE
26 December 2022